Memories

of

Newport

Part of the

Memories

series

Memories

of

Newport

*The publishers would like to thank the following companies for
supporting the production of this book*

Black Clawson International Limited

George Ford & Sons

Graham & Company Limited

AG Pell & Sons Limited

Solutia UK Limited

St Regis Paper Company Limited

Tovey Brothers

First published in Great Britain by True North Books Limited
England HX5 9AE

© **Copyright: True North Books Limited, 1999**
This edition reprinted as softback, 2002

ISBN 1 900463 59 8

Text, design and origination by True North Books Limited
Printed and bound by The Amadeus Press Limited

Memories are made of this

Memories. We all have them; some good, some bad, but our memories of the town we grew up in are usually tucked away in a very special place in our minds. The best are usually connected with our childhood and youth, when we longed to be grown up and paid no attention to adults who told us to enjoy being young, as these were the best years of our lives. We look back now and realise that they were right.

So many memories - perhaps of the war and rationing, perhaps of parades, celebrations and Royal visits. And so many changes; one-way traffic systems and pedestrianisation. New trends in shopping led that to the very first self-serve stores being opened.

Through the bad times and the good, however, Newport not only survived but prospered. We have only to look at the town as it is today to see what progress has been realised and what achievements have been made over the last 50 years. Newport has a history to be proud of - but more importantly, a great future to look forward to, into the new millennium and beyond.

Contents

Events & occasions

These ladies (and chaps) have got up early to grab a good seat for some event or another, and we suspect that it could well be the Royal visit in 1937. Here they are, dangling their legs from the window ledges of the bank in Bridge Street; from their perch they will be able to see over the heads of the crowd which will, as the morning progresses, begin to throng the pavement in front of them. Looking back, one can't help thinking that in those days people dressed up more than they do now. Whenever we went to the theatre or the pictures or the park, we dressed up; Sundays meant Sunday best; and if we were going to see the Queen then we definitely wore our best frock and hat. The sheen on the dangling legs suggests that we have got our silk stockings on, too. Meanwhile the lad in the dark jacket and light trousers is doing a good trade in 'favours' - little ribbons to be pinned on the ladies' dresses, in this case no doubt red, white and blue. Such entrepreneurial spirit would have assured him of a good career as a 'spiv' before he was many years older - except that of course everybody in Newport was too patriotic to get involved in the black market. Weren't they?

Both pictures: The coronation of King George VI gave everyone a chance to declare their loyalty to the new sovereign, and it was party time in Newport. High Street along with the rest of the town was hung with banners and flags, and red, white and blue garlands decorated every lamp post. Not only were there the official events to look forward to, but there were the many street parties, dances and fireworks parties to enjoy. Along with the rest of Britain, the tight-knit communities around Newport let their hair down and went to work on giving the kids a good time. So the ladies donned their aprons while their menfolk carried the kitchen table and dining chairs out into the street. Every family chipped in and contributed towards the loaves of bread, packets of butter (or dare we suggest margarine?), sandwich fillings, jellies, cakes of every kind - and not forgetting the gallons of tea and crates of pop that would be needed. We draw a veil over the kind of beverage that the parents would need once the children were all tucked up in bed....

King George VI went on to take his place as perhaps Britain's most well loved monarch. During the second world war the compassionate attitude of the King and Queen - today our much revered Queen Mum - established them both in everyone's affections. Many were in tears when they heard of the King's death from lung cancer in 1952; he had been a heavy smoker for many years. King George VI was genuinely mourned by the whole nation.

Both pictures: Miles of bunting and garlands turned Commercial Street into a riot of colour when King George VI was crowned on 12th May 1937. Newport was determined to be loyal to the new sovereign, and patriotic flags flapped gaily in the breeze from every available flagstaff. In the event the monarch being crowned was not Edward VIII, who Britain had expected to reign after the death of King George V, but his younger brother. Albert, Duke of York, had been hurled unexpectedly into the kingship he had not been trained for when his older brother, who had been King for a mere 325 days, renounced the throne on 10 December 1936 for American divorcee Wallis Simpson, 'the woman I love'. Edward was well-liked for his natural charm and became known as the 'Society Prince', and many must have hoped that he would be allowed to marry the woman he loved. But Wallis Simpson had been divorced twice, the King was Head of the Church of England - and the Church's teaching on divorce was clear. Edward signed the Instrument of Abdication on the 10th December 1936, and the document was witnessed by his three brothers.

The new king was shy and nervous and suffered from an embarrassing stammer (which he later overcame with medical aid and the support of his wife Queen Elizabeth). 'I'm only a naval officer,' he confessed to his cousin Lord Louis Mountbatten on the day he became king. 'It's the only thing I know about.' He had never seen a state paper in his life. But he rose to the challenge, squared his shoulders, and adopted the title of George VI.

Newport is certainly keeping the flag flying in this picture! We believe this scene to have been part of the 1937 Coronation celebrations in Mellon Street. The little girls' costumes suggest that this particular day's events included a Coronation parade; it is a safe bet that there was a party, too, and by bedtime they would be tired out from all the excitement and ready to go to sleep and dream about Kings and Queens and handsome Princes . . . When we were young, Royalty was about as unreal - or as real - to us as fairytales. How could the innocent, fresh-faced youngsters in the front row guess that sixty years hence they would be reading in the tabloids of the far-from-fairytale marital problems and personal tragedies being faced by George VI's grandchildren?

Above: Any guesses what this cheeky band in Mellon Street are up to? It might help to know that that the photo was taken shortly before the Coronation in 1937... They're not exactly painting the town red; in fact, what they are doing is whitewashing the street! Newport was preparing to celebrate in style, with street parties, dances and all manner of events, and the whole town was decked out with red, white and blue for Coronation week. It had been an emotional decade for ardent Royalists. Indeed, the whole nation had shared in the joy of celebrating George V's Silver Jubilee, followed only a couple of years later by sadness at his death; anticipation of the Coronation of Edward VIII had given way to suspicion and doubts as rumours about his attachment to Mrs Simpson began to circulate, and it was both a shock and a relief when his abdication was announced on 10th December 1936. The date fixed for the Coronation remained the same, but it was another Prince who was to be crowned, as Albert, the shy, unassuming younger brother, stepped in to take Edward's place and become George VI. And Newport got the whitewash out to make sure its streets were fit for a King.

Above right: The bunting was out for King George V's Silver Jubilee celebrations, and it is quite clear what the high-light of the celebrations was for the children on this picture - the Tea Party (this particular one was in Dudley Street). Of course, they may well have already eaten half a pound of chocolates each - thousands of free boxes were given out to children at the Athletics Ground; the boxes, which some families have kept to this day, bore portraits of Their Majesties. For those who considered themselves too old for jelly and ice-cream, there was plenty of other entertainment

on offer. Newport's Olympia was putting on 'Royal Cavalcade', 'An array of unsurpassed entertainment talent - in stars'; the Empire was offering 'A Jubilee Variety Programme'; while the Tredegar Hall promised that its '25 Years A King' 'gets you by the throat'. There were sports events, there was a great bonfire on Lawrence Hill, there was revelry; for some it was a day of prayer; and at Gwent Hospital it was the day of the official naming ceremony of the Silver Jubilee Ward. For those who wished to hear a public broadcast of the King's Speech, the Olympia, the Empire, the Tredegar Hall, the Lyceum and the Pavilion had all arranged transmission at 8 o'clock on Monday 6th May. When the highly-respected monarch concluded his speech by echoing Queen Victoria's words on her Diamond Jubilee 38 years earlier: 'From my heart I thank my beloved people. May God bless them' - it really did 'get you by the throat'.

Below: The sun shone as Newport received what, rather surprisingly, seems to be the town's first recorded visit by a reigning monarch, on July 14th, 1937. The new King George VI and Queen Elizabeth began their coronation tour of Wales at Newport, and the occasion coincided nicely with the town's plans to commence work on the new Civic Centre.

The Royal party made its way to the rose garden of St Mary's Lodge, Clytha Park, along a route decorated with flags and thronged with cheering crowds who had turned out in force to catch their first glimpse of the new monarch. This photograph shows the King cutting the first sod on the site, with a silver spade especially made by Messrs Pleasance & Harper. Their Majesties were favourably impressed with the park surroundings and expressed the hope that it would be possible to preserve many of the magnificent trees, commenting that they would greatly enhance the value of the completed project in years to come.

Bottom: The royal couple's second visit to Newport took place under very different circumstances. The date was Friday 31st March 1944, and the main topic for discussion was the war.

A glance at the 1930s

HOT OFF THE PRESS
The years of the 1930s saw Adolf Hitler's sickening anti-Jewish campaign echoed in the streets of Britain. On 19th October 1936 Oswald Mosley's 7,000-strong British Union of Fascists clashed head on with thousands of Jews and Communists in London, resulting in 80 people being injured in the ensuing battle. Mosley and his 'blackshirts' later rampaged through the streets beating up Jews and smashing the windows of their businesses.

THE WORLD AT LARGE
In India, Gandhi's peaceful protests against British rule were gathering momentum. The Salt Laws were a great bone of contention: forced to buy salt from the British government, thousands of protestors marched to the salt works, intending to take it over in the name of the Indian people. Policemen and guards attacked the marchers, but not one of them fought back. Gandhi, who earned for himself the name 'Mahatma' - Great Soul - was assassinated in 1948.

ROYAL WATCH
The talking point of the early 1930s was the affair of the Prince of Wales, who later became King Edward VIII, and American divorcee Wallis Simpson. Faced with a choice, Edward gave up his throne for 'the woman I love' and spent the remainder of his life in exile. Many supported him, though they might not have been as keen to do so if they had been aware of his Nazi sympathies, kept strictly under wraps at the time.

These ladies have found a novel way of extending their line of vision, and are obviously tickled pink with their discovery! All you need to do is get your make-up mirror out of your handbag and hold it up, angling it in the direction of the procession - and there you are, you've

got your own little periscope, and the fact that you're a bit shorter than your neighbour no longer prevents you from getting a good view! From the Union Jacks in the top left corner and draped over the rope in front of the merry crowd, we can deduce that some kind of Royal procession was being awaited; the photograph may have been taken somewhere along the route which King George VI took when he visited Newport at the beginning of his Coronation tour in July 1937.

Both pictures: When Newport decided to offer the Freedom of the Town to Field-Marshal Sir Bernard Law Montgomery, it was departing from tradition in that 'Monty' was the first Freeman without any particular personal connection with the town. However, the Field-Marshal had earned the respect of the people of Newport, of Monmouthshire and indeed the whole nation by his actions during the war, and when it was announced, on Tuesday 26th June 1945, that Field-Marshal Montgomery had accepted the Freedom of the town, there was great rejoicing. 'I deeply appreciate the honour which the Mayor and Council of the County Borough of Newport wish to confer upon me in making me an Honorary Freeman of Newport,' Monty had written. 'It gives me great pleasure indeed to accept this invitation and I look forward to the time when I shall be able to visit you for this purpose.' In fact, Newport did not have to wait too long before the visit could take place; some three months later Monty was aboard a train pulled by an engine appropriately named

The South Wales Borderers, heading for Newport, where a huge crowd was assembled to pay tribute to a great soldier. Men of the Monmouthshire Regiment of the South Wales Borderers formed the Guard of Honour in Station Approach; a full Field Marshal's Guard was mounted; Field-Marshal Montgomery had lunch at the King's Hotel; and all along the route he was greeted and cheered by men, women and children. The official civic ceremony took place in Central Hall, where, on behalf of the Borough, the Mayor presented him with a solid silver casket and scroll, recording the admittance of Field-Marshal Montgomery to the Honorary Freedom of Newport.

There was great sadness at the time of Monty's death in 1976, but he will never be forgotten. His military exploits, particularly in spearheading the Normandy invasion in 1944, have gone down in history, and Newport can look back and remember with pride the day when Monty stood in their midst and accepted the Freedom of the Town.

Both pages: Newport certainly gave the young Queen Elizabeth a right royal welcome when she and the Duke of Edinburgh arrived, on Thursday July 9th, 1953, to start their post-Coronation tour of Wales. She was cheered by crowds some 50,000 strong. The trains into Newport had been packed with people travelling across from all parts of Monmouthshire and South Wales; some had even camped out all night to stake their claim to their chosen spot which would provide a good view of Her Majesty - in spite of the fact that it had been an unseasonably cold, wet night! It was only about a month since the whole country had been in the grip of Coronation fever. Although Newport's own Coronation Committee, which had been responsible for planning the programme of events, was making gloomy noises about not having recouped as much of the costs of putting on the celebrations as they had anticipated (apparently the citizens of Newport had been expected to spend an average of ten shillings a head at the various celebrations, whereas in the event, partly no doubt due to the bad weather, they had spent a mere four shillings a head), and citizens were being warned that rates might have to go up by 5d per head instead of the anticipated 3d, nobody in Newport held this against the Queen! Old and young turned out to see her - and probably the oldest of all was 100 year old Alice Underwood, who afterwards echoed everybody's sentiments when she said that she 'would not have missed it for anything'.

The camera catches few happy smiles in this photograph taken at a Christmas party thrown for the children by ARP personnel during the second world war. The kiddies had a good excuse; tummies were full, Santa's sack was empty, the party was over and it was time to go home. Mum had arrived to help them into their hats, coats and scarves, and at the end of a long day, bedtime beckoned.

Christmas parties meant races and games - musical chairs and pass the parcel and singing games like 'The Farmer's in his Den' and 'Wallflowers'. Then would come the food - the best the ARP could manage on wartime rations. There would be sandwiches, cakes (with icing if they were lucky), mince pies and jelly; these kids would have had a whale of a time. Then, when they were all tired and full of food would come

the moment they had all been waiting for; Santa Claus himself, complete with red cloak, white beard and wellies, would appear to give each child a gift from his sack. One little girl on the left has been lucky enough to be given the fairy from the top of the Christmas tree. What became of the youngsters in the photograph, we wonder, and what kind of lives did they carve out for themselves?

A glance at the 1930s

MELODY MAKERS

Throughout the 1930s a young American trombonist called Glenn Miller was making his mark in the world of music. By 1939 the Glenn Miller sound was a clear leader in the field; his clean-cut, meticulously executed arrangements of numbers such as 'A String of Pearls' and 'Moonlight Serenade' brought him fame across the world as a big-band leader. During a flight to England from Paris in 1944 Miller's plane disappeared; no wreckage was ever found.

GETTING AROUND

At the beginning of the decade many believed that the airship was the transport of the future. The R101 airship, however, loaded with thousands of cubic metres of hydrogen, crashed in France on its maiden flight in 1930. Forty-eight passengers and crew lost their lives. In 1937 the Hindenburg burst into flames - the entire disaster caught on camera and described by a distraught reporter. The days of the airship were numbered.

SCIENCE AND DISCOVERY

By observing the heavens, astronomers had long believed that there in the constellation of Gemini lay a new planet, so far undiscovered. They began to search for the elusive planet, and a special astronomical camera was built for the purpose. The planet Pluto was discovered by amateur astronomer Clyde Tombaugh in 1930, less than a year later.

Both pictures: Many readers will remember what a grand sight it was when the Town Hall clock tower was illuminated for the coronation of George VI in 1937. Apparently an incredible 5,000 or more multicoloured globes, connected by some 2,000 feet of cable, were used to pick out the outline of the tower and turn it into a blaze of light above the town. The special effects department had been busy, too; above the balcony was an intricate kaleidoscopic-effect rosette, while the top of the tower became a great Royal Crown. Illuminations stretched across the streets, too; the Westgate Hotel had the flags out, Marks & Spencer had huge Union Jacks up, its shop windows were ablaze with light - even the bollards seem to be entering into the spirit of the occasion! Looking back, it is as well that we seized the opportunity to light the town up and enjoy ourselves while we could. Within a few years the blackout curtains will be drawn tight to blot out any chink of light that might attract an enemy bomber, smoke-screen vehicles will be parked on street corners to hide the town, and military parades will be not for show, but for real. In 1937 the new King and Queen will visit Newport on his Coronation tour in a blaze of lighthearted publicity. Their next visit, in 1944, will be unannounced, and will be an altogether more serious affair as they tour Gwent to see how it is coping with war. Patriotism means sharing each other's joy in the good times and supporting each other in the bad.

Bottom: The grim expressions on the faces of motorcyclist and pillion are nothing whatsoever to do with their close proximity to the Chief Constable of Newport and worries about worn tyres or failure to display a tax disc; far from it. In fact, the Chief Constable, seen here with the Mayor and Mayoress Councillor and Mrs H H Jones, is about to start the 1961 Road Courtesy Rally, and these are the first competitors, all ready to pull down their goggles and go, go, go!

The photographer seems to have caught the party at a critical moment in the proceedings; the Chief Constable, who is presumably watching for a signal from further down the route, appears to be averting his eyes rather ostentatiously from the dirty, noisy motorbike. However, the young man standing to the rear of the machine looks much more appreciative of the very fine BSA, today regarded as an all-time classic British bike. So everybody smile, please!

Right: Just in case you were wondering - we have looked at this photograph very closely and can confirm that the procession is definitely NOT emerging from the Murenger! This stretch of road has seen countless procession, whether on foot or by civic or Royal limousine. Behind the civic party is Lloyds Bank, with its remarkably insistent series of inscriptions around it

making absolutely sure we all know that it was erected in 1926, that the builders were H J Herbert, the contractors were John Jenkins Ltd, and the architects were Griggs & Vaughan and Percy R Fry. All the inscriptions are waist-high to a grown-up, and one wonders how many children might have stood there fidgeting, either waiting for a procession to pass or for their mothers to stop chatting to their friends, and out of sheer boredom read the inscription over and over again until in the end they have come away knowing how to spell the word 'architect'!

Princess Alexandra had a busy time when she visited Newport on 11th April, 1962. After arriving at the station at around half past eleven, she went first to the Civic Centre where she met representatives of the Girls' Nautical Training Corps, the Women's Junior Air Corps, the Junior Red Cross, and Guide Dogs for the Blind; guide dog Bess got a special stroke from the Princess. She then signed the visitors' book, looked at the murals in the Civic Centre entrance hall and chatted to the artist, Hans Feibusch. Her next stop was St Woolos Cathedral, where this photograph was taken; she was welcomed by the Archbishop of Wales, met

Princess Alexandra opened the Water Board's new treatment works on 11th April 1962

some of the nurses and saw the extension works in progress at the cathedral. The main business of the visit, however, was the opening of the Newport and South Monmouthshire Water Board's water treatment works. During the course of the day a great many local people were presented to her, and she also stopped for informal chats with bystanders. The large crowds which had turned out to see her were so well-behaved and gave her such a warm welcome that the Princess told the Mayor that she thought the people of Newport were 'very friendly indeed,' and later wrote to 'convey her appreciation to all who joined in welcoming her.'

Saturday, 23rd November 197 dawned cold and frosty. All over Newport, rugby fans - including the Mayor - were anticipating the big match between Newport and the Wallabies; and the excitement was not confined to Newport. Special trains had been put on to bring people in from the direction of Blaenavon and Brynmawr, and another special was running from Gloucester to Cardiff. The Australian team fully expected to win, although they were not invincible - they had already suffered three defeats in the tour, one of them in Wales. The Wallabies began the match well, getting balls back from scrum and line-out much more effectively than in their previous games. But as the match progressed Newport, captained by Malcolm Thomas, began to take command. The home side's first try came from Jack Hurrell, after a good run by Ian Ford; the second, scored by Leighton Jenkins, was converted by Norman Morgan; and, with the Wallabies unable to notch up any points in reply, Norman Morgan scored again with a drop goal. So when the final whistle blew it was Newport 11 - Wallabies 0, making it the first match of the tour in which Australia had failed to score. A memorable victory for Newport!

Sporting life

Below: The supporters of Newport Rugby Football Club have enjoyed many a proud and glorious moment since its formation in 1874. Here are just a few of its legendary claims to fame: during the club's first 100 years, more than 100 Newport men played for Wales; in 1921 Newport fielded a team composed entirely of current international players - ten Welsh, three English, one Scots and one Irish (they beat Bristol 17-0); a Springbok head was mounted in the clubhouse to commemorate their 9-3 win over the Springboks in 1912/13; in 1963/4 they were the only side to defeat the All-Blacks during their tour; and their great international players have included Willie Llewellyn, Jerry Shea, 'Bunner' Travers, Malcolm Thomas, Bryn Meredith, David Watkins, Stuart Watkins and Brian Price. This photograph was taken in 1956, a year in which an impressive run of 17 successive victories was finally brought to an end by a 6-3 defeat by a particularly strong South African Universities team in a hard-fought and exciting match.

The cup victory in 1980 was the highlight of an already superb season

Alongside the successes of Newport's great Rugby Club, any football team would find itself a little overshadowed. However, Newport County has had its moments of glory, and one of the most memorable came in 1980 when, having beaten Cardiff and Wrexham on their way to the final of the Welsh Cup, they defeated Shrewsbury and brought the Cup back to Newport. This was the second time they had reached the final, the previous occasion being in 1962/3 when they lost to Borough United. The years in between had been a time of considerable financial worry and doubts over the future of the club; but

when Len Ashurst took over as manager in June 1978 Newport County gained a new sense of direction. Players such as Keith Oakes, Kevin Moore, Tommy Tynan, John Aldridge and David Gwyther were signed up; the pitch at Somerton Park was improved; and their Cup victory in 1980 was the highlight of a superb season in which they had also established supremacy over the high-flying Portsmouth side (2-0 at Fratton Park and 4-3 at Somerton Park) and attracted an average gate of over 5,000. Their promotion at the end of the season, after 18 years in Division IV, was well-deserved.

Wartime

In 1939 Britain's Prime Minister Neville Chamberlain had made his announcement to the waiting people of Britain that '...this country is at war with Germany.' Newport, along with the rest of the nation rolled up its sleeves and prepared for the inevitable. This war would be different from other wars. This time planes had the ability to fly further and carry a heavier load, and air raids were fully expected. Air raid shelters were obviously going to be needed, and shelters were built on open places across the town.

By the time war was declared an army of volunteers of both sexes had already been recruited to form an Air Raid Protection service. At first ARP personnel were unpaid volunteers but when war broke out in September 1939 they became paid staff. It was their job to patrol specified areas, making sure that no chinks of light broke the blackout restrictions, checking the safety of local residents, being alert for gas attacks, air raids and unexploded bombs. The exceptional work done by Air Raid Wardens in dealing with incendiaries, giving first aid to the injured, helping to rescue victims from their bombed-out properties, clearing away rubble, and a thousand and one other tasks became legendary; during the second world war nearly as many private citizens were killed as troops - and many of them were the gallant ARP wardens.

At the beginning of the war Sir Anthony Eden, Secretary of State for War, appealed in a radio broadcast for men between 17 and 65 to make up a new force, the Local Defence Volunteers, to guard vulnerable points from possible Nazi attack. Within a very short time the first men were putting their names down. At first the new force had to improvise; there were no weapons to spare and men had to rely on sticks, shotguns handed in by local people, and on sheer determination. Weapons and uniforms did not become available for several months.

In July the Local Defence Volunteers was renamed the Home Guard, and by the following year were a

force to be reckoned with. Television programmes such as 'Dad's Army' have unfortunately associated the Home Guard with comedy, but in fact they performed much important work. The Guard posted sentries to watch for possible aircraft or parachute landings at likely spots such as disused aerodromes, golf courses on the outskirts of towns, local parks and racecourses. They manned anti-aircraft rocket guns, liaised with other units and with regular troops, set up communications and organised balloon barrages.

Other preparations were hastily made around the town. Place names and other identifying marks were obliterated to confuse the enemy about exactly where they were. Notices went up everywhere giving good advice to citizens on a number of issues. 'Keep Mum - she's not so dumb' warned people to take care what kind of information they passed on, as the person they were speaking to could be an enemy.

Older folk will remember how difficult it was to find certain items in the shops during the war; combs, soap, cosmetics, hairgrips, elastic, buttons, zips - all were virtually impossible to buy as factories that once produced these items had been turned over to war work. Stockings were in short supply, and resourceful women resorted to colouring their legs with gravy browning or with a mixture of sand and water. Beetroot juice was found to be a good substitute for lipstick.

Clothes rationing was introduced in 1941, and everyone had 66 coupons per year. Eleven coupons would buy a dress, and sixteen were needed for a coat. The number of coupons was later reduced to 40 per person. People were required to save material where they could - ladies' hemlines went up considerably, and skirts were not allowed to have lots of pleats. Some found clever ways around the regulations by using materials that were not rationed. Blackout material could be embroidered and made into blouses or skirts, and dyed sugar sacks were turned into curtains.

Both pictures: Seen here posing for the camera (left) and assisting with air-raid preparations (above), these Basque youngsters had been evacuated from their homes during the Spanish Civil War. In early 1937 Franco's army, with assistance from Nazi Germany, had begun a programme of systematic aerial bombardment on the Basque region, because of its support of the left-wing government who favoured devolution. The National Joint Committee for Spanish Relief had secured permission from the Britain's Home Secretary for 4,000 Basque children to enter Britain, and as no financial aid was forth-coming from the Government the NJC had undertaken to raise ten shillings per child per week for maintenance. The children, aged between five and 15, arrived on the ship 'Habana' on 23rd May 1937, accompanied by 95 women teachers, 120 female helpers and 15 priests, and were initially accom-modated at an emergency camp set up outside Southampton. From there they were dispersed to various centres which were able to offer them accommodation - Catholic homes, private houses, Salvation Army centres and Ministry of Labour Training Camps. Cambria House, Caerleon, was one of two homes in South Wales, the other being Sketty Hall, Swansea. A former workhouse, Cambria House was able to take around 50 youngsters. Although in some places there were a few teething problems - in Brechfa some boys claimed they had been picked on, and retaliated by breaking windows and threatening villagers with knives, prompting the newspaper headline 'Put all these Basques in one exit' - in general the children settled in well, and, as can be seen here, became part of the community. The children performed Spanish and Basque songs and dances in towns and villages up and down the valleys, and the football team at Cambria House beat some of the best schoolboy sides in Wales. When the troubles were over, the children were gradually repatriated; Cambria House was in fact one of the last to close. The Basque people have a cultural and perhaps racial affinity with the Celts. Basque is apparently unrelated to any other European language, and its people have a strong sense of indepen-dence. Today they enjoy limited autonomy. And, who knows, perhaps Basque children today are still hearing from their grand-parents the story of how, when they were young, they were sent to Caerleon, in far-off Wales . . .

The very small boy wielding the very large pickaxe probably wishes he was ten years older, then he could be a soldier and go and sort Jerry out . . . As it is, he's putting his energies into filling sandbags, along with fellow Newport schoolboys and teachers. It's a hot job for a sunny day, and it is reassuring to note that the hole they are standing in is in the grounds of the Royal Gwent Hospital, so if anyone is overcome by the heat, or gets their foot in the way of a

pick, there will be a sympathetic nurse on hand. Sandbags had a multitude of uses, and you could never have too many of them; civic buildings all over Wales and England relied on piles of sandbags to protect them from bomb damage.

Many shopkeepers stuck tape onto their windows in a criss-cross pattern, so that if the window did shatter, the tape would hold the pieces together to some extent and so reduce the risk of flying glass inflicting injury on occupants or passers-by.

Both pictures: 'Little chaps collect the scrap' was the message given out by this cheerful band of youngsters from Raglan Street whose door to door collection of saucepans, old mangles, tin baths, buckets and lading cans had resulted in this creditable pile of scrap metal *(below)*. Their efforts certainly merited this group picture, and they were happy to erect a Union Jack and pose with their spoils for the photographer. When people were asked to donate their iron and scrap for the war effort, there was an overwhelming response from those who wanted to see their old bikes and railings turned into Spitfires and Hurricanes. The appeal went: 'The war is driving Hitler back, But here's one way to win it. Just give your salvage men the sack And see there's plenty in it.' The scrap collection made for the Mayor's Fund resulted in a fine collection of coffee and tea pots, candlesticks - and a vehicle number plate, DAX 20 *(left)*. People had no way of knowing that their sacrifice was largely in vain, and that little of the scrap metal collected during the campaign would ever leave the scrap yards.

During the war, the public were asked at regular intervals to contribute to one worthy cause or another, whether it was in giving their aluminium saucepans and tin baths, donating their odd sixpences and shillings or giving clothes, books and food to organisations such as the Red Cross and the RVS. The war effort prompted much rivalry between local firms; the larger ones might raise £20,000 for a Wellington Bomber (to be repaid after the war), while small companies might manage to get a couple of thousand pounds together to pay for an aeroplane wing. Collections in public houses were more modest, aspiring to £30 for a sub-machine gun or £138 for a 2,000lb bomb. A donation from an individual with a few coppers to spare might be 6d for a rivet or perhaps four shillings for a hand grenade.

Many towns and cities actually 'bought' Spitfires for £5,000; a list of contributors to the war effort was read out over the wireless every day after the evening news.

Both pictures: *The threat of gas was a very real one during the second world war; during World War I thousands had suffered from the deadly, all pervasive mustard gas used by the enemy. So, at least at the outset of World War II, the nation's attention was focused on the importance of protection. The provision of gas masks was seen as a priority.*

A number of types of masks were used during the war. In addition to the civilian's masks two other types were used by civil defence workers. One of these had a rubber ear-piece so that the wearer could use the telephone, and the other was a heavy-duty mask with a supply of oxygen. It was important that police officers and Civil Defence workers, who were in a position of authority, should know exactly how to use the masks; an instructor from the Home Office came to Newport to tutor police officers in their use (below).

Even before war was declared, millions of gas masks had already been manufactured, and as they were delivered to towns and cities around Britain, Civil Defence workers passed on their knowledge of how to use them. Not surprisingly, children were often frightened by the fearsome look of the gas masks, and the very young ones were given blue and red 'Mickey Mouse' masks complete with ears. Babies under two were provided with special gas helmets. Notices posted everywhere reminded people to carry their masks with them, though it was not compulsory under the law. Some cinemas and theatres, however, refused to admit people who did not have their masks with them. The notice 'Hitler will send no warning - so always carry your gas mask' emphasised the danger.

This decontamination squad, looking rather sinister in gas masks and protective gear, are 'cleaning up' Serpentine Road (right) - a practice run for the clean up procedure after an air raid.

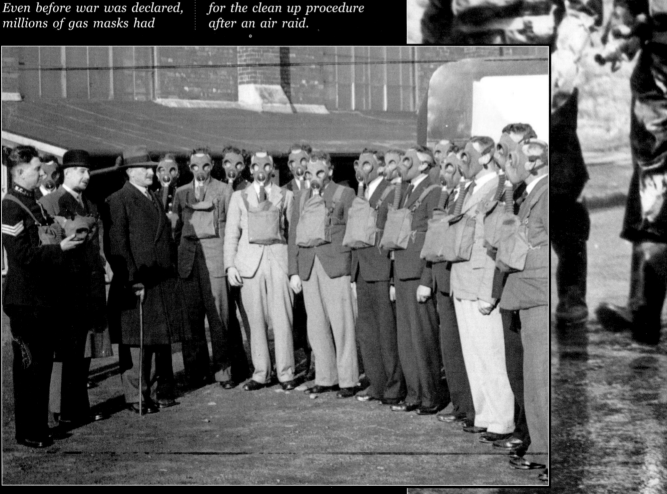

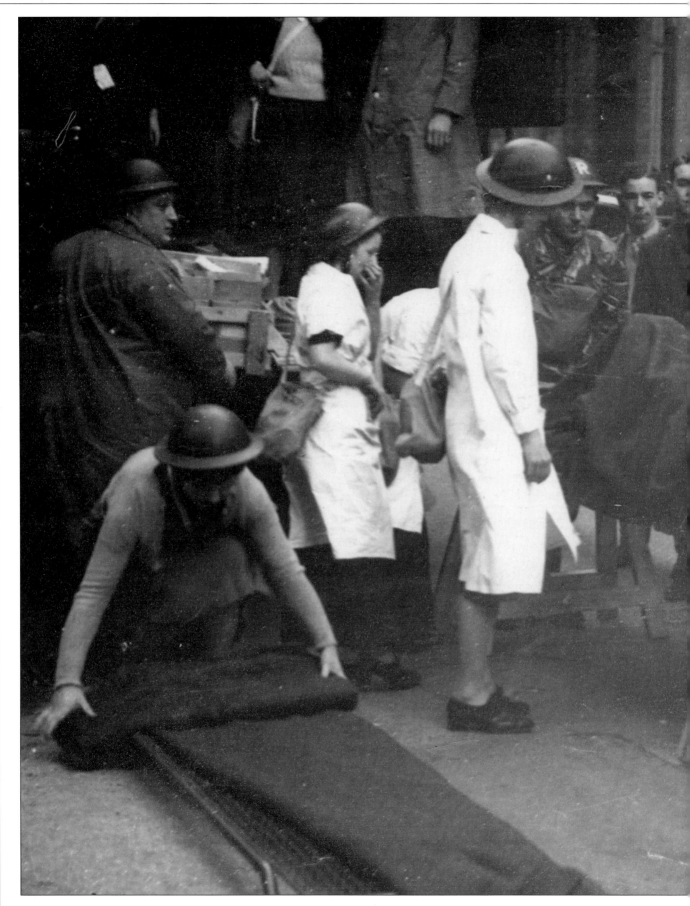

The date of this photograph is given as 11th March 1940, and judging by the expressions on the faces of the rescue squad and the bystanders it seems likely that the casualties being treated on this occasion are real, although details of the incident are not known. Sometimes, of course, scenes such as this were set up as a training exercise. One such rehearsal was the so-called Battle of Newport, staged on Sunday 31st August 1943. This massive, realistic war exercise involved Special Constables, firemen, wardens, first aiders, the WVS, the Home Guard, not to mention fifth columnists and saboteurs, among others.

A glance at the 1940s

HOT OFF THE PRESS

At the end of World War II in 1945 the Allies had their first sight of the unspeakable horrors of the Nazi extermination camps they had only heard of until then. In January, 4,000 emaciated prisoners more dead than alive were liberated by the Russians from Auschwitz in Poland, where three million people, most of them Jews, were murdered. The following year 23 prominent Nazis faced justice at Nuremberg; 12 of them were sentenced to death for crimes against humanity.

THE WORLD AT LARGE

The desert area of Alamogordo in New Mexico was the scene of the first atomic bomb detonation on July 16, 1945. With an explosive power equal to more than 15,000 tons of TNT, the flash could be seen 180 miles away. President Truman judged that the bomb could secure victory over Japan with far less loss of US lives than a conventional invasion, and on 6th August the first of the new weapons was dropped on Hiroshima. Around 80,000 people died.

ROYAL WATCH

By the end of World War II, the 19-year-old Princess Elizabeth and her distant cousin Lieutenant Philip Mountbatten RN were already in love. The King and Queen approved of Elizabeth's choice of husband, though they realised that she was rather young and had not mixed with many other young men. The couple's wedding on 20th November 1947 was a glittering occasion - the first royal pageantry since before the war.

During the course of the day those taking part practised or helped others practise putting out fires, digging people out of bombed buildings, catching spies - in fact the whole range of war-time skills were put to the test. And next morning everyone was back at work again, having given up what was probably their one day of rest. Still, that was war.

Below: On Wednesday 9th October, 1940, a low-flying enemy bomber broke through an anti-aircraft barrage and scattered high explosive and fire bombs over the Pill area. One blast ripped into the Alexandra Dock Hotel, which immediately became the scene of chaos seen on this photograph as part of the structure collapsed, with the falling masonry trapping several people. Rescue workers lost no time in mounting a rescue operation to dig out those buried in the wreckage, but in spite of their efforts three people were killed. The rescuers were afterwards praised for their gallantry, and eight of them were singled out for especial recognition, including Detective Constable Charles Cook who received the George Medal, and PC Edmund Wetter and Mr Joseph Draper who both received the OBE Civil Division Medal.

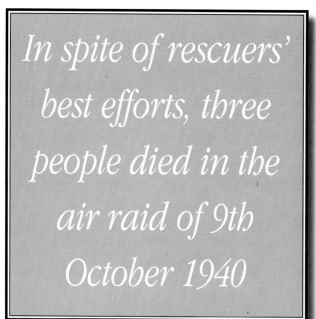

In spite of rescuers' best efforts, three people died in the air raid of 9th October 1940

Right: The pile of rubble and the shored-up building tell their own tale; it is small consolation to those who lost their homes, their businesses and their loved ones to tell them that Newport did not suffer as badly in the war as many other British towns and cities. The unlucky ones here are New York Life Insurance Company and Greenhouse & Scrivener, but with true Welsh spirit they have lost no time in doing what many another firm up and down Britain had to do - found temporary premises and opened up for business as usual. The notices in the window direct shoppers looking for hats, scarves or other accessories to Greenhouse & Scrivener's temporary showroom just opposite, on the first floor, while New York Life Insurance has moved to temporary offices in 12 Skinner Street. It must have been a worrying time for insurance companies, though....

Below: 'You go in there, look, down that hole . . .' Wing Commander E J Hodsall, Inspector General of the Home Office ARP Department, is visiting Newport to inspect ARP precautions, and is being shown an air raid shelter in the car park by a delegation which includes Councillor R S Tyack, chairman of the Newport ARP Committee, the Borough Engineer Mr W C West, and the Chief Constable. An early census in Newport had identified 11,500 households requiring domestic air raid protection. Two thousand Anderson shelters were installed within the first couple of months, and thereafter the lucky families were kept very busy bailing them out after it had rained. Morrison shelters were also installed. Many shelters were made here in Newport; but it is recorded that the ship Trelawney delivered 7,000 tons of Anderson shelters which, by strange coincidence, had been manufactured at the works of John Lysaght in Newcastle, Australia, by ex-employees who had emigrated there. Newport suffered its worst air attack of the war in the early hours of 1st July, 1941, when more than 30 people died and many were injured.

Right: Eyes right! The Air Training Corps is marching past Newport Town Hall, and the Mayor and assembled officers take the salute. During the second world war military parades became an accepted part of life, and were a real morale-booster. Children loved the excitement of the rousing bands and the marching soldiers, and the parades undoubtedly made the average person in the street feel in touch with the military and the progress of the war. So the men buffed their buttons and polished their shoes, and everybody's hearts swelled with patriotic pride as they marched past. Mothers glowed to see how wonderful their sons looked in uniform, and girls blushed at how handsome their young men looked in uniform, and somehow we managed to concentrate on the glory of the moment and forget about the tears just round the corner.

Right: This mobile canteen was a generous gift from non-English Argentine railway staff on the Buenos Ayres Great Southern Western and Midland Railways to the National Fire Service in Newport - and the Mayor, Cllr W G Rudd and his party sample the first mugs of tea brewed up in the new urns.

During the second world war, mobile canteens must have been a cheering sight to the National Fire Service, bringing workers a cup of tea and a much needed break as they battled to clear rubble, rescue people trapped in debris and bring fires under control. The drivers and volunteers manning the mobile canteens themselves often worked to the point of exhaustion to bring relief to working parties around the town.

During the war the National Fire Service took on the control of all civic fire brigades, and women as well as men worked for the NFS. As the war progressed, firewatching became a compulsory duty, and all men between 16 and 60 were called on to organise a fire-watching rota. Later on women between 20 and 45 joined them.

Below: Looking as though he can't wait to get a Nazi in the sights of this Bren gun is Newport's Mayor, Alderman J R Wardell. The occasion was a national recruiting campaign held at the Corn Exchange in 12th July 1939. The previous year Adolf Hitler had signed the Munich Agreement and Britain's Prime Minister, Neville Chamberlain, made the mistake of trusting him. Many, however, had no confidence in Hitler and couldn't believe in Chamberlain's assurance of 'peace in our time', and they went on preparing for a war that they still saw as inevitable. The defence of the nation was of paramount importance, so local air raid precautions organisations were established in every district, and air raid wardens appointed and trained. The Home Office prepared a booklet entitled 'The Protection of your Home against Air Raids' which was sent to every home in Britain. It encouraged every home and family to play an active part 'if this country were ever at war'. A section was provided inside the front cover for the head of the household to record the position of the nearest wardens' post, the first aid post, and the name and address of their warden. Britain finally declared war on Germany on 3rd September 1939.

doing manual work in factories. Nobody denied that they did a marvellous job, but in many cases the general assumption was that as soon as the war was over and the men were back home, the genders would resume their traditional roles - the woman would once again be the homemaker, the man would be the breadwinner, and everything would be back to normal. But, as we now know, this did not happen; the modern working woman was here to stay.

Top: Triumphant smiles all round - these ARP messenger boys have just completed their ride to Llantrisant, near Usk. Just because you were too young to join the army, it didn't mean the ARP couldn't use you - if you were a boy, that is; little girls weren't expected to develop big muscles, but there were still plenty of things they could join in with, such as collecting scrap, picking blackberries, knitting comforters for the troops and helping Mother with the housework, especially if she went out to work. The government had a slogan for everything, and for children it was 'Keep them happy, keep them safe'. The little chaps shown here are happy and safe, and useful too - but just hang on a minute, what was that message they were supposed to remember . . .?

Above: By 1942 Newport was quite used to listening to the tramp of boots up and down its streets. On this occasion it is not boots but shoes which are marching in step, and the ladies in them are the women of the ATS - the Auxiliary Territorial Service. The salute is being taken by the Mayor and assembled officers on the steps of the Monmouthshire County Hall in Pentonville. The war changed our lifestyles. Ordinary women found themselves taking on all kinds of new responsibilities, putting on uniforms, driving buses and ambulances and

The Home Guard performed a valuable service throughout Britain

Although near the end of the queue when equipment and uniforms were given out, the Home Guard nonetheless took its duties very seriously, training with broomhandles while they waited for bayonets to become available and evolving into a competent and dedicated force. Many of them, of course, had relatives - brothers, sons, cousins and friends - in the trenches; so they followed the progress of the war attentively, both for personal reasons and in order to anticipate what the Home Guard would be called upon to do in the coming weeks.

Bottom: An example of recycling, late 1930s style - this World War I tank used to stand near Livingstone Place, in Maindee, and is here being cut up for scrap. The British Army had pinned great hopes on its new weapon, the tank, in the first world war. Shipped to France in crates marked 'water tanks', a clever ploy to confuse the enemy, these armoured vehicles were first used on 15th December at the Battle of the Somme. Their tracks meant that they could travel over terrain that wheeled vehicles could never have crossed, but they were not as reliable as had been hoped because of fuel shortages and mechanical breakdowns. In the second world war, tanks were still used but engineers turned their attention to designing airborne fighting machines . . . and the rest is history.

Right: This RAF van is on the lookout for young men with a head for heights and a taste for adventure . . . Touring South Wales on a recruiting campaign, the van is here seen parked in Commercial Street, Newport. 'We shall fight with growing confidence and growing strength in the air,' Winston Churchill proclaimed in 1940. And we did; the RAF, the youngest of the three armed services, acquired a daredevil image - night bombing raids over Germany, hair-raising flying stunts and dog fights in the air. Mothers and girlfriends lay awake at night listening to the drone of the engines, and worrying, knowing that some would limp home on one engine, and some wouldn't come back at all. The RAF wasn't an easy option; standards were high, and flight training, especially as the war progressed, was very intensive. Of course, not everyone who joined the RAF ended up on active service; ground technicians and engineers were also neeed - less dangerous and less glamorous, but vital nonetheless.

Around the town centre

Here is the view of Newport which used to greet travellers approaching the town from the east. This photograph takes us back to the days of the horse and cart and the tram, but it was not until 1970 that radical redevelopment brought us the big roundabout that stands at the west side of the bridge today. Some readers will remember the Shaftesbury Cafe site as Jay's furniture store. The row of shops here used to include John Hall's tools and the Singer sewing machine shop, which sold dress patterns, buttons and all manner of other dressmaking accessories as well as actual sewing machines; while Boyds used to be on the corner, and further along by the river was HFE's builders merchants. There has been a bridge on this spot for at least 700 years; the Normans are thought to have constructed a timber bridge soon after the castle was built. The stone bridge seen here was built in 1800 and drastically widened in 1866. A traffic census on 15th August 1925 counted 6,131 motor vehicles, 1,447 tramcars, 6,951 cycles, 1,133 horse-drawn vehicles, 81 horses, 241 handcarts and too many pedestrians to count. A new bridge was needed. During construction, all traffic - including the electric trams - used a temporary bridge which was placed alongside the old stone one, and in this way disruption was kept to a minimum. The new bridge, which cost £250,000, was opened by the Minister of Transport on 2nd June, 1927.

Bottom: Once you could drive both ways, then you could only drive one way, now you can't drive there at all . . . Once we had Philips seed merchant, Liptons, Halfords, Wernetts the jewellers, the Electricity offices and the Town Hall . . . the details change, but Commercial Street has always been a thriving shopping street, with a good selection of shops. The angle of this photograph emphasises the classic styling of the upper storeys of the buildings; the ones on the left with their arched first-floor windows and decorative masonry are for the most part still in excellent decorative order today, and are a credit to their owners. Certainly the town centre buildings have stood to benefit from pedestrianisation, now that they are not constantly subjected to the grime and vibration caused by passing traffic. Let us hope that the Westgate Hotel building will soon be restored to its former glory and given a new lease of life.

Right: The presence of Tram Number 11 and Tram Number 35, with a Leyland Titan TDI at the bus stop, waiting to set off for Malpas, dates this picture to the early 1930s. That was an era when Westgate Hotel was flourishing. Not only is it a building of considerable architectural merit - it is listed Grade II - but it also makes an interesting contribution to Newport's history. During its construction in 1886, excavations for the new foundations revealed a passage under Stow Hill, remnants of a stone spiral staircase and a medieval gateway - this could have been the site of a West Gate, although there is still debate as to whether or not Newport had a town wall. The Westgate Hotel building is also famous for its Chartist connection. An earlier Westgate Hotel stood on the same site before being demolished to make way for the new, and the original pillars were incorporated in the present edifice, where they now stand inside the entrance instead of outside. In each pillar is set of small holes, which are a legacy of bullets fired during the Chartist riots of the 1840s . . . or so the story goes!

Above: Fluctuations in a country's economy are inevitably reflected in the fortunes of its docks. Falling imports are bad news to dockers. During the 60s the docks were thriving; 1966 was the best year since 1931, and Newport's highest recorded level of imports came in 1968, when it reached 3,779,044 tons. That figure included 3,038,794 tons of iron ore and 195,364 tons of oil and spirits. Within a dozen years or so, imports of both these products had dwindled to virtually nil; Port Talbot took over the handling of all iron ore shipments to South Wales in 1975, and in order to survive Newport had had to actively look for ways to diversify. To add to its troubles, the Newport Shipbuilding and Engineering Company, which had provided employment for many local people, had announced its intention to wind down its activities, and had ceased taking on new work in 1971.

Right: Transporter Bridge is a Grade II listed structure and a unique and valuable part of Newport's heritage. From the moment construction began almost a century ago, everybody in the area took a keen interest in it, and although in financial terms it never really paid its way, we would not be without it! The foundation stone was laid by the Mayor on November 8th, 1902, and the bridge was opened by Lord Tredegar on September 12th, 1906. Designed by the French engineer Francois Arnodin, the bridge represents a masterpiece of lightweight engineering, with a main span of 645 feet and towers which stand 242 feet above road level. The original cost was £98,000; running costs, however, have proved rather high, recently reaching some £160,000 a year. Various refurbishment works were carried out during the early 1990s, and a re-opening ceremony was held in December 1995, attended by Clare Short, MP, the Shadow Secretary of State for Transport. We understand that Transporter Bridge is assured of an important place in the Council's future plans for this area of the riverfront. The Americans once made an offer for it, but Transporter Bridge belongs to Newport. Illuminated, it makes a wonderfully picturesque sight; and no visitor to the area should miss the opportunity to cross it - an unforgettable experience, and at 50p an absolute bargain!

The presence of all the traffic gives High Street an unfamiliar feel . . . But pave it over and replace the buses and trucks with trees and seats, and it's not so very different after all - although at the time of writing the Post Office building at the end is hidden behind scaffolding and plastic sheeting and undergoing a complete transformation inside, whilst its distinctive exterior will be preserved. The photographer would

have been standing just by the entrance to the market to take this shot, and the picture shows that the canopy had not yet been added. The easily-recognisable pointed white gable towards the far end on the left is of course

Ye Olde Murenger public house, the oldest pub in Newport and a Grade II listed building. The building beyond it on the corner was a bank for many years, up until relatively recently.

A glance at the 1940s

MELODY MAKERS
The songs of radio personalities such as Bing Crosby and Vera Lynn were whistled, sung and hummed everywhere during the 1940s. The 'forces' sweetheart' brought hope to war-torn Britain with 'When the Lights go on Again', while the popular crooner's 'White Christmas' is still played around Christmas time even today. Who can forget songs like 'People Will Say we're in Love', and 'Riders in the Sky'?

INVENTION AND TECHNOLOGY
Inspired by quick-drying printers' ink, in 1945 Hungarian journalist Laszlo Biro developed a ballpoint pen which released viscous ink from its own reservoir as the writer moved the pen across the page. An American inventor was working on a similar idea at the same time, but it was Biro's name that stuck. A few years later Baron Bich developed a low cost version of the pen, and the 'Bic' ballpoint went on sale in France in 1953.

SCIENCE AND DISCOVERY
In 1943 Ukrainian-born biochemist Selman Abraham Waksman made a significant discovery. While studying organisms found in soil he discovered an antibiotic (a name Waksman himself coined) which was later found to be the very first effective treatment for tuberculosis. A major killer for thousands of years, even the writings of the ancient Egyptians contain stories of people suffering from tuberculosis. Waksman's development of streptomycin brought him the 1952 Nobel Prize for Medicine.

A view of Lower Dock Street in times gone by. The building on the right which looks rather like a castle used to be the Territorial Army headquarters. Mellon Street, opposite, used to take you to Newport Library, and on the way you would pass the Neptune and the Borough Arms. Gus Roberts paper shop was along here too; readers may remember the tragic

murder which took place here, making the headlines and shocking all those who knew him. In the background, rising up with quiet dignity, is the old Town Hall. When this was opened in 1843, with a grand ball held to mark the occasion, there was no clock tower. It was during the 1880s that the business of the town outgrew the space available; an extension was built and opened in 1885, and it was at this stage that the impressive clock tower was added. Its place as a focal point on the horizon of this part of Newport has now gone to that rather different structure, Chartist Tower.

Above: Traffic lights have replaced what now seems, from a quick glance at this photographic record, to have been an excessively complicated road layout. The Odeon is now Capones American Bar; the building opposite, on the corner of Caerleon Road, was once, if memory serves, the Alexandra nightclub, and is at the time of writing a fitness centre. The funeral home which used to stand on the corner has gone, but instead we have the Inland Revenue offices, a place still regarded with considerable apprehension by some, in spite of tax inspectors' efforts to cultivate a more user-friendly image. The foundation stone for the Cenotaph was laid in April 1924, and in June, in front of a huge crowd and a massed parade of troops, Major General Lord Treowen unveiled the completed monument. No-one could have foreseen, then, that only two decades later it would become necessary to add another line to the inscription. This now reads: 1914-18, 1939-45, Their memory endureth for ever.

Above right: It is April 1955, and the South Wales Argus is still sharing its frontage with the Army Recruiting Office. - cunningly placed with the pedestrian crossing leading straight through the door, so any of Newport's young soldiers-to-be would feel obliged to take a deep breath and march across the road smartly and confidently, just in case the recruiting sergeant happened to be looking out of the window! In fact, National Service continued to be obligatory until the end of that decade, and in subsequent years there were still those who held rigidly to the opinion that it should never have been stopped, asserting that army discipline was the best cure for juvenile delinquency. These days Newport's youth passes through the doors of that particular building with a much lighter heart and without all the soul-searching that preceded the taking of the King's Shilling; that same building is now, of course, The Old Monk public house.

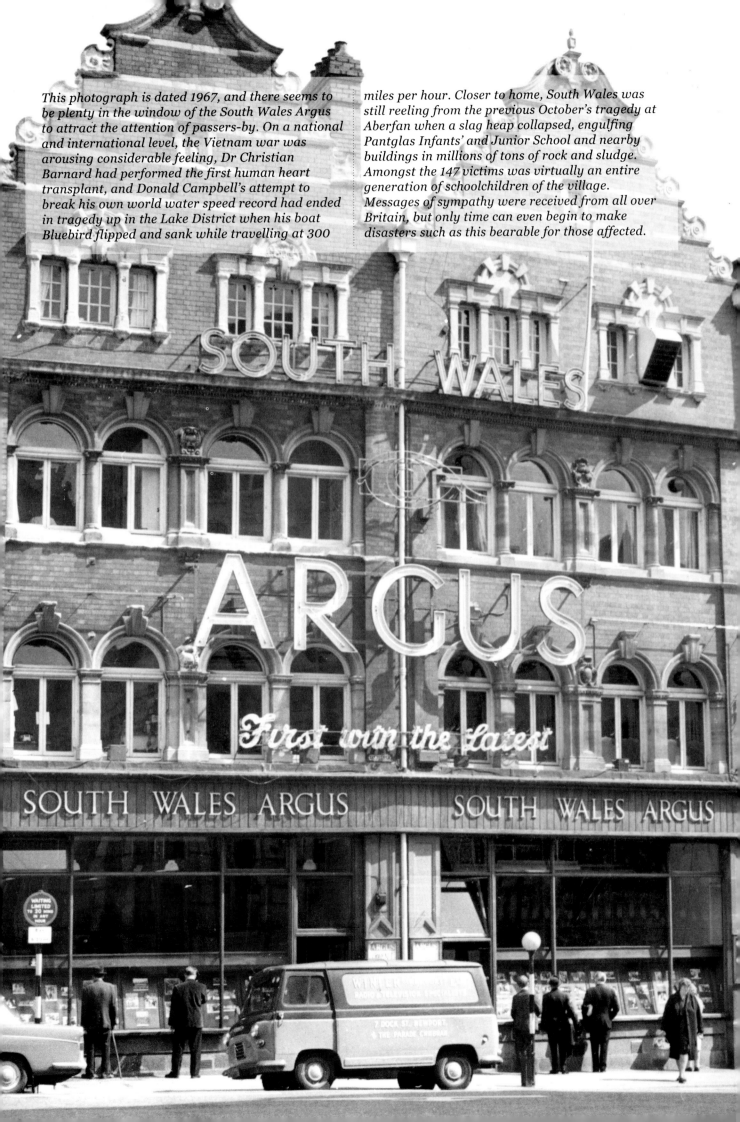

This photograph is dated 1967, and there seems to be plenty in the window of the South Wales Argus to attract the attention of passers-by. On a national and international level, the Vietnam war was arousing considerable feeling, Dr Christian Barnard had performed the first human heart transplant, and Donald Campbell's attempt to break his own world water speed record had ended in tragedy up in the Lake District when his boat Bluebird flipped and sank while travelling at 300 miles per hour. Closer to home, South Wales was still reeling from the previous October's tragedy at Aberfan when a slag heap collapsed, engulfing Pantglas Infants' and Junior School and nearby buildings in millions of tons of rock and sludge. Amongst the 147 victims was virtually an entire generation of schoolchildren of the village. Messages of sympathy were received from all over Britain, but only time can even begin to make disasters such as this bearable for those affected.

Commercial Street in the 1950s had plenty of familiar names, though not necessarily all in familiar places. Samuel's clock is there, with a sign beneath it which proclaims 'H Samuel for Good Watches' - and a quick cross-check between Samuel's clock and the Town Hall clock confirms that the two are in agreement. Opposite Samuel's is Boots, with Barclays Bank next door, and further down, beyond the Town Hall and with its sign just visible above the top of the parked

truck, is Saxone. The Town Hall would no longer have been in use for council business when this picture was taken; its official role had been transferred to the Civic Centre in 1950. A century or so earlier, it had no doubt seemed an excellent idea to site the new Town Hall as centrally as possible. However, it was this which ultimately brought about its demise as the commercial centre of the town grew up around it and left it no room to expand.

Above: Although the scene at the crossroads is quiet enough at the moment, there will be a surge of traffic from town as soon as the lights change. Once the trend was set for a rapid rise in car ownership, it was inevitable that the Old Green area would have to undergo radical redevelopment to cope with the increase in traffic. Dual carriageways made life easier for the motorist; then there was the pedestrian to think about. In the years between the wars a staggering 120,000 people were killed on Britain's roads, prompting Mr Leslie Hore Belisha, the Minister of Transport, to introduce the first pedestrian crossings; the first crossings were marked out by studs, and they still had to wait a few more years before they got their stripes. Even then, persuading people to use them was another matter. There have been various nationwide initiatives over the years to educate children into crossing roads safely. Some readers might have joined the Tufty Club when they were at school. More recently we have had the Green Cross Code. But clearly the best solution is not to have to cross the road at all; Newport's town planners thought of that, and provided us with subways in the Old Green redevelopment scheme.

Right: The SALE signs in Noel's shop window no doubt help to explain why High Street is so jammed full of buses, cars and shoppers as far as the eye can see. The shoppers all have their overcoats on, so we would guess this picture was taken on a Saturday afternoon during the January sales. The policeman in the foreground, with his back to the camera, can do little more than stand there until the congestion sorts itself out, and perhaps keep a stern warning eye on the car which is apparently disgorging its passengers outside Mac Fisheries, totally disregarding the No Waiting sign. (Speaking of Mac Fisheries, collectors of trivia might be interested to know that the Mac Fisheries chain originated in 1921 when Lord Leverhulme set up a project to help impoverished Scottish crofters by turning them into fishermen and bought 300 shops to sell their fish!) When we look at this photograph it is not difficult to see why the town planners decided upon pedestrianisation for the centre of Newport; shopping there is a much less stressful experience now.

Remember the 60s, when the bus station used to be here? The buses have gone, and the cars have gone, and so has the leather shop which used to be on the corner; but the fruit and veg barrow in the forefront of the picture - was it A A Wright's? - makes us realise just how long we have been buying our fruit and veg from this very spot. Now we no longer have to dodge the traffic, and we can take the weight off our feet and admire the statue of the little piggy that went to market. While statues have proliferated in

recent years, Newport fortunately managed to resist the temptation to fill the town with tower blocks. Still, there are enough, and some would say more than enough; Chartist Tower and Olympia House, which from this angle seem to merge into one, score few points in many people's opinion when compared to the grand and often quite ornate architecture preserved from earlier times, which we can still admire on the upper storeys of the buildings on the right of the picture and in other parts of town.

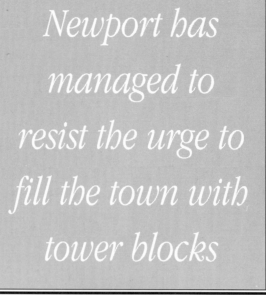

Newport has managed to resist the urge to fill the town with tower blocks

On the move

The electric tramway began to take over from horse-drawn trams on Thursday 9th April 1903, with the introduction of a service between Pill and Lysaghts work entrance on Corporation Road. The Chepstow Road section was the second route to be opened, becoming operational on 27th May. The Caerleon Road section opened in June, the Malpas Road section the following month, and the Stow Hill route was introduced later. The fare between the Chepstow Road terminus (on the borough boundary) and the Pill terminus was 2d, but the early morning and evening trams had special cars for workmen, with a fare of 1d regardless of how far they went. Trams served Newport well for almost 30 years, but with the arrival of the 1930s motor buses began to take over. The Chepstow Road trams were among the first to go, replaced by buses on 18th August 1830. Newport's very last tram of all left Westgate Square at 10.50pm on Sunday 5th September, 1937 - for the record, it was Tram Number 51, driven by Mr J Evans. Tram Number 52, seen in this picture, went to Matthews & Wards scrapyard at the end of 1937.

If you walk along the frontage of this building (now the indoor market) to your right, and round the corner, off the picture, you will find a plaque with the date 1934. Prior to this, the stretch of High Street between Griffin Street and Market Street used to be narrower, and blockages regularly occurred when lorries had to pass each other at this point. So the projecting frontages were pulled down, and replaced by a new arcade entrance to the market - Crown Arcade, now Royal Chambers - and a new row of shops with offices above, set well back from the road. The department store Hills & Steele originally occupied these spacious premises, which, by the time this photograph was taken, had became Great Universal Stores; it then became British Home Stores, and many readers will remember the fire which broke out there on 5th November 1951, damaging the upper floors and ruining thousands of pounds worth of

A glance at the 1950s

WHAT'S ON?
Television hit Britain in a big way during the 1950s. Older readers will surely remember 'Double Your Money', 'Dixon of Dock Green' and 'Dragnet' (whose characters' names were changed 'to protect the innocent'). Commercial television was introduced on 22nd September 1955, and Gibbs SR toothpaste were drawn out of the hat to become the first advert to be shown. Many believed adverts to be vulgar, however, and audiences were far less than had been hoped for.

GETTING AROUND
The year 1959 saw the development of the world's first practical air-cushion vehicle - better known to us as the hovercraft. The earliest model was only able to travel at slow speeds over very calm water and was unable to carry more than three passengers. The faster and smoother alternative to the sea ferry quickly caught on, and by the 1970s a 170-ton car-carrying hovercraft service had been introduced across the English Channel.

SPORTING CHANCE
The four-minute mile had remained the record since 1945, and had become regarded as virtually unbreakable. On 6th May 1954, however, Oxford University student Roger Bannister literally ran away with the record, accomplishing the seemingly impossible in three minutes 59.4 seconds. Bannister collapsed at the end of his last amazing lap, even temporarily losing his vision. By the end of the day, however, he had recovered sufficiently to celebrate his achievement in a London night club!

Christmas toys. Arson was suspected, as an unusually high number of fires occurred in Newport around that time. BHS subsequently moved to the site of the old Town Hall, where it still is now, and its former premises became an extension to the market. So much for the Universal Stores building itself; of course, what everybody looking at the picture will be wondering is, what are all those people waiting for? Wouldn't you like to know . . . (So would we - though we guess they're off on a works outing!)

Above: Was this a novel form of breakdown recovery? A form of early competition for the AA or RAC, perhaps? Part of a carnival parade? Or was the horse pulling this open-top motor car along High Street as a rather off-beat advertising gimmick? A fascinating story must lie behind this little charade, though the details have unfortunately been lost in the mists of time. We have no date for the photograph, but we can make a guess at the 1930s.

Private cars were quite rare at that time in comparison with today, when owning a car (or more than one!) is quite the norm; 60 years or so ago, cars tended to be owned by the more affluent. Motoring, however, was becoming a popular hobby, and between the end of World War I and 1930 the number of cars on Britain's roads increased from around 200,000 to more than a million.

Above right: This is the second railway station on this site. Newport's original station building was a low, single-storey building. It had two platforms, and there was a separate booking office on each of them. Station Approach was then created to link the new station with the middle of town; this happened shortly after the opening of the South Wales Railway on 18th June 1850. In order to follow the most direct route it was necessary to demolish two properties on the High Street, one of which was a residence belonging to John Frost, famous for his role in the Chartist uprisings. The original plans included an imposing stone archway into Station Approach from High Street, but for some reason this was never built - which is rather a shame, as one can imagine that, on the occasion of Royal visits or other civic occasions, a procession leaving the station and winding its way down beneath an arch would have made a grand spectacle. In the early 30s the old station was replaced by the multi-storey brick-built station which we have today; this photograph was taken shortly after the new building was completed.

Old photographs of buses and bus stations can often be dated by the advertisements on display: cigarette advertisements with no Government Health Warning, adverts for products such as Soako or Omo or Dilly Duckling Cough Pastilles which our parents or grandparents remember better than we do - but in this case we have an even more helpful clue. The very eagle-eyed (or those equipped with a magnifying glass) might be able to make out that, below and to the left of the advertisement for Elkes Biscuits on the side of the Caerleon bus, the square white poster reads: For Peace Sake Join Civil Defence. So petrol rationing would soon put the owners of private cars back onto public transport; while the taxi firm Montax converted their vehicles to run on gas, which they carried in a large bag on the roof. Necessity is the mother of invention.

Our parents and grandparents may remember adverts for Soako or Omo

Bird's eye view

The puff of steam from the train crossing the railway bridge gives an indication of the length of time that has elapsed since this photograph was taken; it pre-dates the Old Green redevelopment by some considerable time, and there is not a tower block to be seen, but there are nonetheless a number of familiar landmarks to be picked out on this aerial view of Newport. Just right of centre is the distinctive copper dome of the old Newport Technical Institute; an inscription by the entrance tells us that the foundation stone was laid on 24th June 1909 by the Mayor, Graham W White Esq, JP, and the architect was C F Ward. At the time of writing this fine building is standing empty, waiting to learn what the future might hold. The area of land upon which it was built used to be an orchard, cottage and nursery, until it was consumed by fire in 1897. Rodney Parade, running along the east (here, top) side of the Usk and leading to the rugby ground to the right, used to be the site of a drill hall and parade ground, hence its name.

Below: *The development of every settlement is influenced by its geographical features, and so the River Usk has played a significant role in the development of Newport. For a start, every town with a river running through it has to work out a strategy for getting across it. Newport has had a permanent crossing where Newport Bridge is today for many centuries; a bridge is believed to have existed at around the time that the castle was constructed, a new bridge was built in 1800, and the present one in 1927. Add to this the cost of our famous Transporter Bridge and the George Street Bridge, and the expense is considerable. Then, rivers bring the problem of pollution. In 1936 the town recognised that it had a problem with rats and declared an official Rat Week; over the year 1,179 rats were poisoned. In recent years, although the Usk still gives environmentalists some concern, great improvements have been made and recent developments have brightened up the area along the river.*

Right: *Here we see George Street Bridge under construction. The more far-sighted of Newport's citizens had predicted the need for another river crossing some 50 years earlier; the replacement of the old stone bridge by the existing Newport Bridge following a traffic survey in 1925 had alleviated the problem to some extent, but as readers will remember it continued to be a traffic bottleneck. After the second world war campaigning began in earnest, and the pros and cons of various proposals and counter-proposals were hotly debated while traffic queues grew and grew. Finally a design by engineers Mott Hay & Anderson met with approval, the Ministry of Transport agreed to grant £1million towards the cost, and the diggers moved in. Once begun, work progressed at an impressive rate and the new bridge was completed within 21 months - and this in spite of the exceptionally severe winter of '63 which caused unavoidable disruption and delay. The Mayor, Councillor Trevor Vaughan, was finally able to declare the £2million George Street bridge officially open on April 9th, 1964.*

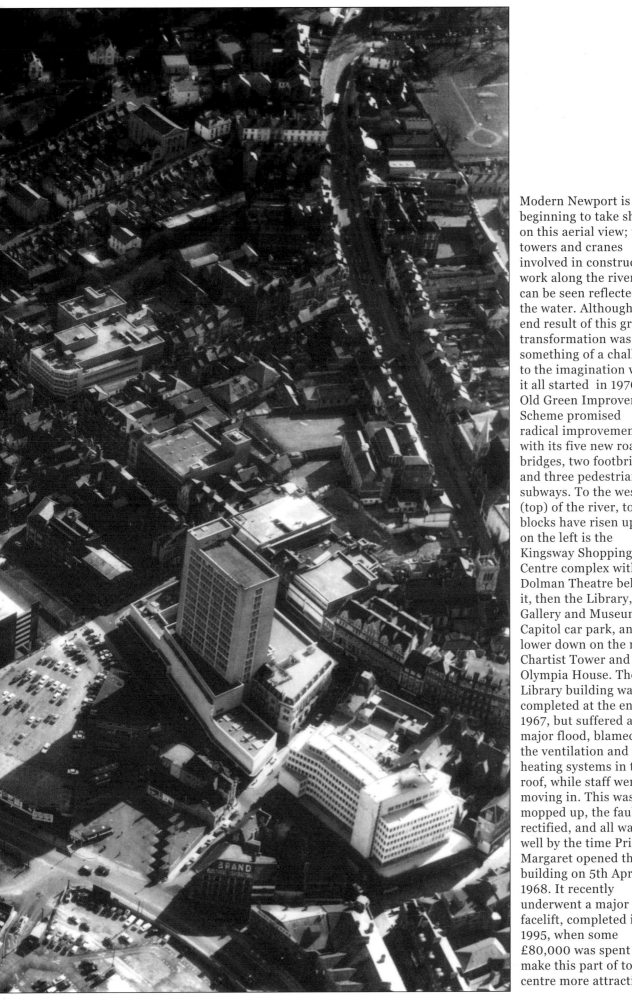

Modern Newport is beginning to take shape on this aerial view; the towers and cranes involved in construction work along the riverside can be seen reflected in the water. Although the end result of this great transformation was something of a challenge to the imagination when it all started in 1970, the Old Green Improvement Scheme promised radical improvements, with its five new road bridges, two footbridges and three pedestrian subways. To the west (top) of the river, tower blocks have risen up; up on the left is the Kingsway Shopping Centre complex with the Dolman Theatre behind it, then the Library, Art Gallery and Museum, Capitol car park, and lower down on the right Chartist Tower and Olympia House. The new Library building was completed at the end of 1967, but suffered a major flood, blamed on the ventilation and heating systems in the roof, while staff were moving in. This was mopped up, the fault rectified, and all was well by the time Princess Margaret opened the building on 5th April, 1968. It recently underwent a major facelift, completed in 1995, when some £80,000 was spent to make this part of town centre more attractive.

Shopping spree

Once it was the latest in menswear that was displayed in the ample window area provided by the shop on the corner of Skinner Street and High Street; on this picture it is ladies' fashions, with Noel's taking over the site which used to be Burton's. At the far end of the street the banner across the road is informing us that St Woolos is holding its Annual Fete, while the bus nearest the camera provides us with some more contemporary 1950s reading with its adverts for Pell's Old English Mints, and A E Hughes & Son's radio and television shop. Another clear sign of the times is South Wales Builders' Supply Co Ltd's call to 'modernise your bathroom' - the post-war DIY boom would have been in full swing by now, and young couples all over Newport would be astounding the older generation - and perhaps driving their neighbours to distraction - with their sudden enthusiasm for putting up fitted units and cupboards and shelves, giving their living rooms a fresh lick of paint, and brightening up their bathrooms with new coloured bathroom suites and maybe the latest low-flush WCs. Home improvements were becoming affordable thanks to DIY, and living standards generally were on the up.

Bottom: A glimpse of Griffin Street in 1959, taken from an elevated viewpoint - how many readers knew that there was a 'manipulative practitioner and chiropodist' above Cecil's, ready to treat your corns? Ladies of all ages are going about their shopping. In the days before supermarkets and as many free plastic carrier bags as you want, you never dreamed of setting off to go shopping without your trusty shopping bag in your hand. The boat-shaped wicker baskets like the one held by the lady looking in Cecil's window were very popular in the late 50s and early 60s. In those days all a shopping bag had to do was hold your shopping; it did not also have to act as a secure, crime-proof contraption with zips and clasps on every compartment, and if you kept your purse on top of your shopping so that you could get at it easily when you needed to pay your bus fare, you did not feel you were inviting muggers to strike.

Right: Burton's, with its distinctive curly lettering, is occupying the prime site on the corner of High Street and Skinner Street in this photograph. Montague Burton's good quality menswear has been a firm favourite with the gentlemen for many generations, and the chain grew until virtually every town and city in Britain had at least one branch. The story goes that when soldiers were demobbed after military service they were given vouchers to be fitted out in civvies at Burton's. They went along to the nearest branch and were kitted out in what was then termed 'the full Monty' - and that is the origin of the phrase which has in recent years come to mean something very different from a full suit of clothes! A little further down on the same side, high up, is another familiar sign - that of Pearl Assurance, with its large, plain lettering. We tend to think of 'corporate image' as being a new concept, but long-established businesses were quick to catch on to the value of displaying their name in an easily-recognisable style, so that shoppers in an unfamiliar town could easily spot familiar stores from the other end of the street.

At work

A young miner strides off to work with a jaunty smile - and the only indication that a war is on, is the little box under his arm which contains a gas mask. Gas attack was what the country dreaded, and great pains had been taken to ensure that every citizen was issued with a gas mask; demonstrations were held on how to use them, and we all knew that we must carry them with us at all times. Even babies had them. Of course, as the war progressed and no gas ever materialised, we all became a bit more casual about our gas masks; and the boxes, until they fell to bits, made such handy containers for our sandwiches . . . so although the official line is that this young man is carrying his gas mask, it might yet turn out to be a couple of spam rolls!

Left: This action shot of Linotype operators at work at the South Wales Argus was probably taken during the 1930s. Linotype machines such as this are museum items today, although a few are still in use; at the time of writing a mere handful of newspapers still operate them, and some are kept for specific purposes such as imprinting names onto pencils. The Linotype operator turned hand-typed copy into the lead slugs used in the printing process; it was a highly-skilled job - and very well paid. The machinery got very hot, as it incorporated a furnace to melt the lead, and the operators did not have the advantage of the modern ergonomically-designed workstation! In recent years newspaper production methods have advanced rapidly. What would these skilled and experi-enced compositors have made of today's state-of-the-art colour printing technology, running at ever-higher speeds? No doubt they would have been impressed, but they may well have pointed out, too, that at the end of the day it's the quality of the news that counts.

Above: During the 30s, journalists' tools of the trade were pen and paper instead of computer technology. It was also a more male-dominated profession than it is today. This photograph of an office at the South Wales Argus, stark and austere as it is by today's standards, is not without charm. You can imagine the atmosphere of intense concentration, the faint whiff of tobacco in the air and the slight scratch of pen on as the journalists scribble out their stories, making sure that they are 'first with the latest'. The newspaper on the desk bears the headline 'The Bereaved Queen', which could well be a reference to Queen Mary; King George V died in 1936, and his widow lived on until 1953. If this is indeed 1936, there will be plenty of Royal scandal to report on in the coming months as Edward VIII's liaison with Mrs Simpson becomes public knowledge.

British made paper from Sudbrook Mill

On the South East coast, in the shadow of the second Severn crossing, stands Sudbrook Mill, part of the St Regis Paper Company Limited. In 1957 when it was first built Sudbrook Mill was Britain's first chemical wood pulp mill. Today it is the only semi-chemical fluting mill in the UK; in the present era when all other mills use waste paper or imported pulp, St Regis Paper Company Limited has a mill that continues to make a high grade fluting paper, known throughout the paper industry as 'Primaflute', for the packaging sector.

Paper makers need a reliable supply of raw materials. Above all it is vital that they have easy access to plenty of water. Sudbrook Mill is particularly fortunate in this respect, as next door to the Mill is the pumping station for the Severn rail tunnel. When the tunnel was dug in the late 19th century, it struck an underground spring which the pumping station had to pump back into the River Severn. Sudbrook Mill was subsequently able to enter into an agreement which allows it to tap into this supply, thus providing 14 million litres of water every day.

The 40 years since the mill was built have seen many changes, both in the paper industry at large and in Sudbrook Mill itself. The mill has changed hands and changed name, its field of operations has been extended and its plant has

Below: *An aerial view of the site taken during the 1980s.*

been updated, representing a substantial investment over the years; but the commitment to quality has remained constant.

The first owners, Wiggins Teape & Company Limited, laid the foundations for a process much smaller than that which has developed over the years. The company built a pulp mill to convert home-grown hardwood timber into bleached pulp for its own use, using ash, beech, birch, elm and oak from the Forest of Dean, South Wales and the West Country. The use of only home-grown hardwood resulted in a special woodpulp, called Gatecel, which gave particular characteristics when blended with other raw materials in the papermaking process. When the mill started up, an output of some 20,000 tons of bleached pulp

Left and below: *The logs are converted into 'chips' ready for the semi-chemical plant to further reduce the raw material into fibres for the paper making process. This used to be an open air, labour intensive job with the employees having to work all hours in all weathers.*

a year was envisaged. By the mid-60s supplies of hardwood were being brought in from many parts of Southern England and output had risen to nearly 30,000 tons.

Unfortunately, a glut in the worldwide bleached pulp market during the 60s had led to a drop in the value of bleached pulp; and it was in response to this challenge that the mill's first change in direction came about, which in turn led to the first change of ownership.

In 1967 Ashton Containers Limited, a member of the Mardon Packaging Group, purchased the pulp mill. With bleached pulp becoming less profitable, other related markets were explored, and it turned its attention to the expanding market for corrugated containers. This was a viable option as the raw materials and the processes used at the pulp mill were well suited to the production of corrugating medium. It was a courageous move for Sudbrook Mill to change to producing semi-chemical pulp for the manufacture of fluting paper - the corrugated part of a cardboard box - and with the addition of a paper mill and a power plant, the mill could

be transformed into a modern integrated pulp and paper complex. New buildings were erected, new plant was installed, and an intensive training programme was organised to retrain the workforce on the new machinery; supervisors were sent to America to learn to operate the machines, and paper machinemen and rewindermen trained at mills in Cardiff, Bristol and Holland. By 1969 the new Paper Machine was fully integrated with the pulp mill. The site became known as Ashton Paper Mill, and little more than a decade after the mill had first begun producing bleached wood pulp, it had successfully switched to the production of fluting paper.

Today Sudbrook Mill is Britain's only chemical wood pulp mill

Top: *Sudbrook Pulp Mill workers in 1958. From left to right, back row: Tom Stowe, Norman Arnold, Glyn Hazel, Len Waters, Pat Bladon, John Vitte, Doug Jenkins, Gerry Jackson, Fred Chesterman, Les Howells, Phil House, Albert Vaughan, Dave Stocke, Bob Scott and Tony Hudson. Front row: Pete Coles, Les Watkins, Eric Hunt, Eric Watkins, Glyn Lovell, Doug Lewis, Jock McShane, Walter Cook, Rowland Edwards, Eddy Dimmock, Tom Wilshire, Eddy Lovell, Len Rutten and Alec Harrison.*

The paper machine has not changed in basic design since it started up and made its first sheet of semi-chemical fluting in January 1969, although major advances in technology have resulted in vastly enhanced productivity. 'Benjamin', as the machine is affectionately known, was designed to make 60,000 tonnes per annum. Now, following substantial investment in new machinery to feed the machine and new electronic hardware to control it, Benjamin produces 140,000 tonnes per annum.

Hardwood arrives at the mill in the form of logs up to ten feet in length and 24 inches in diameter. These logs have to be converted into 'chips' which the semi-chemical plant can reduce into the fibres used in the paper making process. Converting the logs into 'chips' used to be a labour-intensive process carried out in the open air, and in order to keep

Left and below: *Benjamin.*

the machine fed employees had to work all hours in all weathers. In 1995 a new Chipper Plant was installed, and this revolutionised the process. Logs are put onto a sorting log deck where they are washed and aligned, then dropped down a chute into a rotating 12-knife chipper. After passing through the disc, the chips are sorted; any oversize chips go back through the process, and chips of the correct size are conveyed away from the Chipper House onto the chip pile. The sawdust is fed into an incinerator that also supplies steam to power the process. This system works so efficiently that two men operating the machine for six hours can supply sufficient chips to keep Benjamin supplied for a day.

The chips are conveyed up to the pulp mill where they are 'cooked', using steam and chemicals (hence the name 'semi-chemical fluting'), which

Above and facing page: A machine reel of Sudbrook Fluting (above) weighs 10 tonnes and is slit and rewound (facing page) to the customers' requirements before being stencilled and labelled.

reduces the chips into fibres for the paper making process.

Hardwood fibres account for 65 per cent of the composition of the paper. The other 35 per cent is made up of recycled corrugated cardboard. This is supplied by a sister company, Severnside; it is broken down in hydra-pulpers and passed through mechanical processes which break it down to fibres, and is finally mixed with the wood pulp before being passed to the paper machine.

The Mill has been part of the St Regis Paper Company Limited since 1983, with the company now operating as a subsidiary of David S Smith Holdings. Sudbrook Mill is one of eight mills which, with their combined capacity of around 900,000 tonnes per annum, make St Regis the UK's biggest paper maker. Last year some 15 per cent of this total output consisted of semi-chemical fluting produced by Sudbrook Mill. Three-quarters of Sudbrook's annual output is destined for the UK market, and the remaining 25 per cent is exported.

Ever since the mill first opened on this site, it has provided welcome employment opportunities for the local community. St Regis Paper Company pursues an active programme of liaison work with local schools. For many youngsters, the first introduction to working life takes the form of 'work experience' at Sudbrook Mill, and many of these subsequently become full-time employees. There is a strong culture of staff loyalty within the company; it is not unusual for employees to remain at the mill for all their adult lives, from starting their careers right through to retirement. This loyalty is an important factor in the Mill's continuing success; the improvements in the Mill's performance have been put down to their hard work and their willingness to adopt the new technologies which have been introduced.

Many local school children gain their first work experience at Sudbrook Mill

Sudbrook Mill has played an important part in Newport's economy for the past 40 years, and will continue to do so; and it also has another claim to fame which cannot go unmentioned here. It occupies a site of great historic interest, standing on land that is guarded by a Roman fort. St Regis actively co-operates with CADW, the Welsh Monument Agency, to ensure that the ancient structure is preserved and maintained, and often plays host to groups of archaeologists investigating its embankments. Who knows, perhaps the great conquering spirit of the Golden Age of Rome is still alive somewhere in the foundations; and if it is, it will surely approve wholeheartedly of the tenacity, perseverance and sheer hard work which has brought St Regis Paper Company the success it enjoys today.

With 70 'firsts' to its name, this firm will never take second place!

Younger readers will have no recollection of Westgate Works on East Dock Road, Newport, being anything other than the busy, thriving Black Clawson engineering factory. Older readers may remember that up to 1976 it was W A Baker; but only those with first-hand knowledge of the firm's activities will remember the days when W A Baker specialised in architectural ironwork, or will have been aware that the connection with Black Clawson was first established during the early 50s. This connection was sealed by their amalgamation in 1957. However, the two companies, each of which has a long and fascinating history, both retained their own names until 1976. In that year the firm changed its name to Black Clawson International Limited, W A Baker Foundry Division, Westgate Works, thereby officially establishing Black Clawson's presence in Newport.

From then on, this company's development has played an important part in Newport's economy, not least by providing jobs for local people. As it is now just half a century since Westgate Works turned its attention to general engineering, this seems an appropriate time to look back over the history of the two businesses and trace the events which led to the formation of the company which we know today.

In 1853, 34 years before the original Westgate Works was built, two Americans teamed up to grind rolls for the Miami Valley Paper Company in Ohio, USA. Their names were Peter Black and Linus Clawson, and when soon afterwards they installed their first machine line at a small mill in Rockdale, Ohio, with a view to breaking into the paper machine market, the story of the Black Clawson Company had begun.

Below: 1967 protective clothing! This suit was used when pouring molten metal in the Cylinder Foundry.
Bottom: *Black Clawson's Newport site.*

Left: *Pouring a drying cylinder for a paper machine.* **Below:** *The machine shop full of paper machine components.*

1971, the first rubber extruders in 1925, and the first converting equipment for wax paper in 1946. The latter development was produced by the Dilts division, a machine shop in Fulton, NY, set up in 1867 by Frank Dilts, and purchased by Black Clawson in 1940.

Nineteen forty-seven saw Black Clawson established in Great Britain, with the formation of Black Clawson England, in North Cheam, Surrey. The following year a London office was opened; and the year after that Black Clawson England became Black Clawson International Limited, a wholly owned subsidiary company of the Black Clawson Company, USA. Early production of the British company was limited to Stock Preparation equipment, but within a few years it had extended into Converting Paper and Board machines, with Bowaters UK and Townsend Hook & Company among its early customers. The majority of its manufacturing was carried out by W A Baker & Company, and in 1957, just ten years after establishing itself in Britain, Black Clawson purchased W A Baker's entire share capital.

Ten years on, Black Clawson was exporting equipment not only all over America, but all over the world. Part of the secret of its success lay in its commitment to research and development, and this is something which has not changed; the three basic philosophies and principles that Peter and Linus established have remained central to the firm's activities. These, in today's terminology, are: to set new standards, to answer customer needs, and to build nothing less than superior quality converting equipment.

Always synonymous with innovation, Black Clawson has pioneered many of the inventions that have become 'standards' in the paper and board industry, such as the twin wire vertical paper former, the continuous pulping machine, and the first paper machine to break the 1000 fpm speed barrier. In total it can claim more than 70 converting and pelletising firsts, including the first coating lines for video and computer tape in

However, the company was to remain based in the London area for another decade and a half before moving its entire operation to Newport. Its London office had already moved premises numerous times; originally located in Catherine Street, it had then moved to larger premises in the Haymarket, then to

Maddox Street, and then to two buildings in Savile Row. In 1960 the Engineering Department moved into office space in New Oxford Street, and in the same year the Converting division moved into manufacturing facilities in Woolwich. Three years later all offices moved to a new, purpose-built office block in Croydon; and it was not until 1971 that BCI finally transferred all its divisions to Newport, where they joined the Unidac Division which had been set up there the previous year to design and supply electrical drive equipment and instrumentation. It was to be another five years before the name of Black Clawson appeared above the Westgate Works in Old Town Dock.

The original Westgate Foundry, built in 1887, stood on the site of the old Hope Chapel in Chapel Row, behind Commercial Street. A decade or so previously W A Baker had taken over the business of Mr John Nicholas, Iron Founders, who worked from a site on Dock Street/Skinner Street, and he transferred this business to his brand new foundry in Chapel Row. This became known as Westgate Ironworks, and W A Baker subsequently acquired additional sites, one at the top of Dock Street known as Central Ironworks and one in Commercial Street. Records dating from the early 1900s show the firm as furnishing ironmongers, general iron and steel merchants, founders and ornamental metalworkers. They had a telephone, and they proudly gave their national number in their 1904 catalogue - 40! In 1910 the company was re-formed as W A Baker (1910) Limited, at the new Westgate Ironworks on the Old Town Dock. The original Chapel Row site subsequently became the site of the Olympia Cinema, and is now Olympia

House. Montague Burton Limited now occupy the Commercial Street site.

The Westgate Ironworks were modernised around 1925; the entire premises were re-modelled, with the shops re-planned and laid out to facilitate ease of movement, and the works then consisted of up-to-date cupolas, furnaces, fitting shops and large fencing shops. There was also a fine smithy with 26 forges which was the largest to be found south of Wolverhampton, and was considered amongst the finest in the country. It was during this period that the company produced some of its finest architectural metalwork, and we are fortunate in that many examples are still in existence today.

By 1945 the company had been taken over by the Whitehead Iron & Steel Company, and the brass foundry had been developed for a wide range of non-ferrous work and ornamental craftwork. There was also a renewed demand for architectural metalwork to replace items removed or damaged during the war, and for new post-war building developments. Thos Spittle's old foundry was taken over and absorbed into W A Baker & Company Limited around this time. However, W A Baker's days in the architectural and structural business were numbered; in 1949 they undertook the manufacture of the impressive ornamental entrance gates to the Jefferson Gardens at Royal Leamington Spa, and this was to be their last real architectural contract of merit. From then on they moved towards general engineering, developing

Below: *The pattern shop.*

extensive machine shops and a highly mechanised iron foundry; and, although they could not have known it at the time, the future of the company was assured when the Black Clawson Company became their main customer.

The mechanised iron foundry was later closed down and the steel foundry re-sited in its present location, and during the two decades following the amalgamation of W A Baker with Black Clawson the Westgate Works continued to expand. While the Engineering Shops became completely absorbed in the manufacture of pulp and paper making equipment for Black Clawson, the foundries developed their service to industry with a wide range of ferrous castings, concentrating on the manufacture of carbon, alloy and stainless steel products. In 1974 the Meehanite Foundry was modernised, giving it the capacity to manufacture flake and nodular iron castings, and the Steel Foundry too was equipped with new plant and equipment to extend capabilities in that area.

The change of name to Black Clawson International Limited signified the beginning of an extensive re-development programme which has resulted in vastly increased performance throughout the Division.

Today, the company's core activities remain focused on the design, engineering, manufacture and supply of a range of equipment for the Pulp, Paper, Paper Board, Converting and Plastics Industries. In addition, the Unidac Division designs and supplies sophisticated AC and DC electric drive equipment, process control and instrumentation systems, programmable logic controllers and distributed control systems, and serves the steel and non-ferrous metals industry, materials handling, and the water industry. Westgate Works has also become involved in the design, engineering and manufacture of machinery for the corrugated paper business, which represents a new direction for the Group.

Around 70 per cent of Westgate Work's total production is exported to customers in over 30 countries, and the company received the Queen's Award for Export Achievement in 1988. Three years later its Quality Management System earned it the ISO 9001/BS 5750 Part 1 Lloyd's Register Quality Assurance Standard. The company is now well equipped to face the challenges of the next millennium; as a member of the privately held Landegger Industries (L I Group) its effective presence in the world market is assured, while the skilled local workforce and the management team led by managing director Peter Holloway will ensure the continuation of the long tradition of excellence common to both W A Baker and Black Clawson. And many more generations will grow up in Newport knowing Westgate Works as Black Clawson's busy, thriving factory.

Above left: *Carl C Landegger, Chairman of the Board, pictured at LI Group HQ, Chrysler Building, New York.* ***Below:*** *BCI's first seven-layer barrier film line on assembly at Newport.* ***Bottom:*** *The current Managing Director Peter Holloway, left, with Deputy Managing Director Tony Smith at the Westgate works.*

Respect and compassion for almost a century and a half

In Llanarth Street, Newport, during the mid-19th century, there was an undertaker, and next door a bootmaker. Both were well-established family businesses; the undertaker was Mr Palmer, whilst the bootmakers was run by Daniel Tovey. Daniel Tovey's involvement in funeral directing came about almost by chance: Mr Palmer fell ill, and Mrs Palmer asked their neighbour the bootmaker to assist her. Daniel obliged, and his care and assiduity in carrying out the duties brought an increasing number of requests for him to attend to funeral arrangements personally. The logical consequence was that he should take over the running of the business; and in 1860 he founded Tovey Bros, as a successor to Palmers Undertakers, setting up in premises at nearby Dock Street.

With his reputation already established the business soon enjoyed considerable success. His brother Isaac assisted and in due course the founder's sons George and James joined their father in the business. Tovey's in Dock Street grew, and before long they acquired Central Mews, at number 67 Dock Street, a few hundred yards along from the offices. There, spacious carriage rooms housed a fleet of carriages for all occasions; many of which were built and maintained on the premises. In 1893 it is recorded that there was stabling for over 30 horses, including a valuable stud of Belgian black horses for funeral work.

Around the turn of the 20th century James Tovey, Daniel's younger son, retired; but George's son Humphrey had by this time come into the business. George's death in 1908 left Tovey's in the hands of the third generation. Humphrey was soon joined by his younger brother Percy, and between them they guided the firm through the first world war. During these traumatic years they rendered every possible assistance to the community; one very practical and very welcome way in which they helped was by taking injured soldiers from St Woolos Hospital for trips to the seaside or out to the countryside in the firm's brakes.

The years between the war saw a number of changes. Humphrey died suddenly in 1929 at the age of only 47, and two of his sons, Arthur and Leslie, joined Percy in the business. The firm stopped using horses in 1933; Central Mews was sold, and garaging for the new motor vehicles was created behind the offices, in Union Street. The offices by this time extended across numbers 41,42 and 43 Dock Street, and following Arthur's marriage in 1934 the Dock Street branch was run by Percy and Leslie, whilst Arthur established another successful funeral business in Barry.

Above: *The Central Mews premises at the end of the 19th century.* ***Below:*** *A cortege led through Commercial Street, Newport by Messrs George and Humphrey Tovey in 1907.*

are continuing with the extension and refurbishment of the garages where the prestigious Daimler fleet is kept, and the construction of a new carpenter's workshop and storage facilities. Tovey's are in fact unique in the area in that they employ their own carpenter to make, by hand, solid wood coffins.

As readers who have visited Tovey's will know, it is a fine funeral home, becoming a Grade II listed building in 1997. It is described as a well-preserved example of a 19th century villa in the Greek revival style. The decorative plaster ceilings and the panelled doors, with classical figures and cresting above are particularly worthy of note.

Humphrey Tovey, the fifth generation, entered the business in 1964, the year after Percy's death and Leslie's retirement. It subsequently became impractical to operate two branches; Newport has always been the heart of the business, so the Barry office was closed in 1970.

Nineteen ninety-seven marked Arthur Tovey's 75th year of active involvement in the business, and was also the year in which his grandson James Tovey joined the family firm. Thus for the first time in this business three generations were working together. This is a remarkable achievement, perhaps unique among funeral businesses; and indeed Tovey's is a remarkable business. Committed to providing a personal service of the highest standard, particular to the needs of the individual family and at a reasonable charge, Tovey's continues to offer the people of Newport a family-owned funeral service in an age where the trend is for large corporations to purchase and operate funeral homes. Many generations of local families have been well served by Tovey's, and it is comforting to know that future generations can count on the same compassionate, attentive and high-quality service.

Tovey family tree of funeral directors

(where there are two brothers, each generation is succeeded by the son(s) of the elder brother.

First Generation
Daniel Tovey   Isaac Tovey

Second Generation
George C Tovey   James Tovey

Third Generation
G Humphrey Tovey   Percy J Tovey

Fourth Generation
Arthur H Tovey   Leslie C Tovey

Fifth Generation
Humphrey P Tovey

Sixth Generation
James FP Tovey

During World War II both the Newport and the Barry branches of the firm were called upon to deal with the repatriation of American soldiers who had died in Wales. Repatriation is an aspect of the firm's business for which there is considerable demand today, and Tovey's offer a service both to and from anywhere in the world.

The Newport business remained in Dock Street until the 1950s, when plans for the new Kingsway Centre development resulted in a compulsory purchase order being issued. It was at this point that numbers 9 and 11 Cardiff Road became Tovey's funeral home, subsequently No. 7 was acquired and demolished to create extensive car parking facilities. A major refurbishment and extension programme in the 1990s resulted in the spacious and tastefully-appointed premises where today's clients find comfort and consolation at their time of sorrow. Refinements include a new roomy, air-conditioned service chapel with an organ and music system, private chapels and family rooms. At the time of writing building improvements

Right: *Three generations of the Tovey family. From left to right: James, Arthur and Humphrey.*
Top: *The premises today at Cardiff Road.*

Freewheeling to a successful chemical solution

There are not many places where you can see people walking and cycling across an industrial estate. But this is the case at the site at Corporation Road, where the chemicals company Solutia UK Ltd has its operating plant. As part of the National Cycle Network, a path has been laid across Solutia's land. Cyclists and walkers are free to use it on a route from the transporter bridge to the Caldicot Level and will no longer have to fret about dangers and pollution of road traffic on this stretch of their trip.

South of the cyclepath are 30 hectares (75 acres) of meadow which Solutia intends to allow Gwent Wildlife Trust to manage for nature. Solutia has an active community liaison panel that has also seen involvement in local schools. Regular classroom visits are made to both secondary and primary schools.

Solutia's 324 acre site (131 hectares) incorporates a chemical manufacturing operation which currently makes use of 110 acres (45 hectares) of the site total. It is a strategic location, being only three miles from the centre of Newport and close to the M4 motorway. Near

Right: An aerial view of the site in the early 1950s, prior to expansion. Below: Another view of the growing site from the air taken in 1957.

this confluence of the River Usk with the Severn Estuary, the company produces five groups of industrial chemicals. Over 90,000 tonnes of chemicals are produced each year and are distributed to over 1,000 customers. Exports account for well over half of the plant output, going to about 90 different countries across the globe. There are also manufacturing plants in Belgium and the USA. The products are used in a variety of manufacturing processes. Tyres, paint, detergents and heat transfer fluids all include products of the Solutia range of chemicals.

In those first days of the Newport site the workforce had its own washing and changing rooms which many other companies didn't have. The company has continued to show a commitment to its employees by later replacing these with even more modern facilities. There is also an excellent restaurant. In the past, the old canteen was used as the venue for workers' playtime shows, plays and dinner dances. Solutia today, shows a human face to the industrial world. Changes in working practices, computerisation of process control and developments in such industries as pharmaceuticals have kept the company at the cutting edge of the business. The original focus for Monsanto, in chemicals, began to change to one of cash generation, to allow growth in the 'life sciences'. In September 1997, Monsanto split into two separate companies with Solutia becoming a completely independent chemical company. The name changed, but the intentions to serve the industry and the community have remained. The site has an Environmental Management System which is accredited to ISO 14001 and the company publishes an EMAS Environmental report every year (which is independently verified).

Top left: *Until the 1970s most of the Chemicals were received by rail.* ***Above left:*** *The Combustor installed in 1992 burned nearly 1,300 tons of carbon monoxide and 23 tons of xylene in 1998.* ***Below:*** *Parties of school children are frequent visitors to Solutia for educational tours.*

The company grew as Monsanto Chemicals. There had been chemical operations in North Wales in 1867. The first pure phenol was produced there. Around this time, Lister had begun his work on antiseptics in medicine, as well as in the dyeing industry. Demand grew at such a rate that, by 1900, half of the world's supply of phenol was being produced there. Between the two world wars, the growth of the plastics industry provided another market for Monsanto Chemicals. It had taken over the complete ownership of the plant in 1928. By the time the Second World War had finished, it had become obvious that expansion was needed to keep up with the increasing demands of wider industry. What had been Great Traston Farm near Newport was earmarked as the site that Monsanto needed. The land was flat and close to docks and the railway. The old farmhouse was used as an office until 1979. Construction of the new factory began in 1947 and was soon producing its first detergent, Santomerse in 1949. The 120ft tower of the Lustrex plant dominated the skyline. It is in here that polystyrene production took place.

The company that has chartered the waters of Newport history for over 150 years

E very now and again a community is fortunate enough to have in its midst a distinguished family which, for generation after generation, plays a leading role in civic and business life.

Such a family is the Graham family of Newport, whose contribution to the life of the town over more than 150 years has been immeasurable.

Herbert. Eighteen seventy-two saw his name entered upon the roll of Surveyors for appointment under the Land Clauses Act, and that same year he became Agent for Mr T P Price, MP, an extensive landowner with properties on the east bank of the River Usk, at Newport, in the county of Monmouthshire and in the country of Hereford. Two years later he also became responsible for managing the properties belonging to Mr Morgan Stuart Williams of Aberpergwm, Glamorganshire.

Readers who are familiar with the present-day offices of Graham & Co, Chartered Surveyors and Estate Agents, in St Pauls House, Commercial Street, will be interested to know that the practice was set up by Mr William Graham in 1844 and has been continuously in the hands of the Graham family ever since, having being passed down from father to son. William Graham was born in London in 1823 and, after a private education, took up residence in Newport. Having set up in practice, he rapidly rose to a position of eminence both in his profession and in public life. By 1849 his reputation was such that he was appointed agent for the well-known Clytha Estates of Mr William

Around this time William Graham took Mr William Hitchcox into partnership, and the firm became known as William Graham, Hitchcox & Co, Land Agents, Estate Agents, Architects and Surveyors, Valuers and Auctioneers. Mr Graham's son, William Graham (Junior), had also joined the practice. Meanwhile, William Graham (senior) had become increasingly involved in public life. Among the many positions of civic responsibility which he held during his life were those of Magistrate for the Borough of Newport, High Bailiff of the

Top left: *William Graham, founder of the company.* ***Above centre:*** *William Graham Jnr, JP. FSI.* ***Top right:*** *William Graham, current owner, JP. AM. FRICS.*

County Courts of Monmourthshire (at Chepstow and Usk), Justice of the Peace, member of Newport Town Council from 1857 to 1872, and Mayor of Newport in 1866.

One very significant development with which the practice was involved during the mid-1870s was a project to build a rail connection between an extensive riverside wharf, situated on land owned by Mr T P Price, and the Great Western Railway's lines. Sidings, warehouses, offices and the section of track itself were all designed and constructed by the practice, and it continued to exercise control over the enter-prise. The railway attracted manufacturing and other important commercial ventures to establish themselves on adjacent land, and was thus an important factor in Newport's future growth and prosperity.

During the final decade of the 19th century Messrs William Graham, Hitchcox & Co, with William Graham (Junior) and William Hitchcox as partners, moved to Bank Chambers, above the National Provincial Bank of England. These premises afforded private rooms, drawing offices and general clerks' offices, and provided comfortable accommodation for the draughtsmen and practical surveyors employed by the firm. Both partners were fellows of the Surveyors' Institution, as, indeed, had been William Graham (Senior), founder of the South Wales branch of RICS.

In 1940 the name of the practice reverted to Graham & Co. The firm has occupied a number of different premises during the course of the 20th century. It operated for many years from Midland Bank Chambers in Bridge Street, which it leased. In more recent years the firm has preferred to buy its premises, and retain ownership of the property. Thus it still owns its former offices in Stow Hill, at 114 Commercial Street - which it occupied for some 22 years - and the large town building in Cambrian Road, from where it practised until 1998. St Pauls House, its current home, was completely re-built to the firm's own specifi-cations, and now provides a comfortable suite of offices and has the advantage of possessing its own car

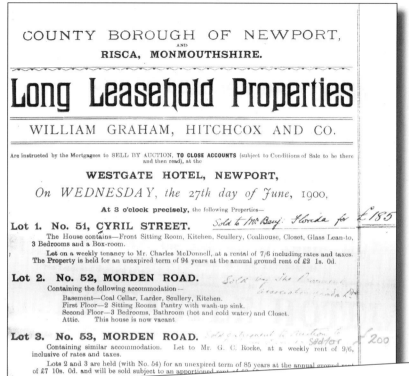

Above: Sales particulars.

park. The ground floor comprises two large retail units which, at the time of writing, are leased to an electrical business and a greengrocers.

It is inevitable that both the form and the substance of the transactions undertaken by the practice should have changed in nature to an extent over the years. However, all credit is due to the practice for the care with which it has preserved its archives; so, though the days of the quill pen, laborious transcriptions and mental arithmetic are long gone, we still have records from those times, which make truly fascinating reading for the historian or for the simply curious.

Thus we can trace the firm through five generations, down to the present William Graham, who has been principal of the family firm since 1970. William Graham is every bit as well known to the people of Newport today as his ancestors were to their fellow townsfolk. He has lived and worked all his life in Newport, and has been appointed to numerous positions of responsibility including Newport Harbour Commissioner, Elder and Trustee of the United Reformed Church (Victoria Road), Deputy Chairman of the Board of Governors of Rougemont School, and past President and Charter Member of the Rotary Club of Caerleon. Married, with three children, William Graham takes an active part in every aspect of community living, from fundraising for charity to politics. This latter sphere is of course very much to the for at the time of writing, with the establishment of the Welsh Assembly and the beginning of a new and exciting era for Wales. It is entirely appropriate that William Graham, whose family has done so much for Newport, should now be involved in making the decisions which will ultimately ensure the best possible future for the Welsh people.

Left: *William Douglas Graham.*
Top left: *William Benjamin Graham.*
Below: *114 Commercial Street.*
Facing page, top: *24 Cambrian Street.*
Facing page, bottom: *St Paul's House.*

The firm that is more than a spare part

The only time the FA Cup went out of England was in 1927. All of Wales knows the answer when it is set as a quiz question. It was the year that Cardiff City won. Amongst the crowd at Wembley that day, clutching his five bob ticket stub, was George Ford. Born in Cardiff in 1907, he worked firstly for Dunlop in his home town. It was as a storeman with Jones 'the Austin people' that he made his first contact with Newport. Sadly, his first wife died as a young woman and he was left to bring up two young sons alone. Hard work did not worry George, nor did grumbling about the raw deal life had served him up hold any attractions. He met the world head on and, in 1954, set up in business for himself as a provider of motor accessories and spares for all makes of cars and vans. Ably assisted by Rose, whom he married in 1955, the business expanded from its first site on Chepstow Road through several on Church Road until a final move brought George Ford and Sons to its present home on Crawford Street, with its 9,000 sq ft of warehousing and the 11,000 sq ft car park. it was one of the first in the business to open on a Sunday. Keen car owners and mechanics often used George Ford's as a meeting place, away from cutting the lawn!

This is a family firm with three generations having been involved in the trade. George was followed by his son, Richard as managing director until 1985 and finally by his eldest son, Joe who still remains as managing director today. They have continued to make sure that a reliable service is always provided to customers who have come to feel that their needs are the company priority. Good links with and technical support from main suppliers like Ferodo, Lockheed, Bosch, Fram and many more main distributorships that George Ford hold have kept them ahead of the rest. With the opening of the Cardiff branch, all of Glamorgan and Monmouth can be covered. In those first days, when the firm began, who could have imagined where it would all lead? From tiny premises, where the amount of stock carried was small and all bills and invoices were hand-written, to the massive computerised site of to-day is the giant leap that began with a single step in the 50s. In fact, George Ford's are very much about people and relationships, and their motto of *Service you can rely on!* is epitomised by the 50 people now employed by the company.

Left: *George Ford, the Company founder.*
Below: *George Ford's motor accessory shop on Chepstow Road in the 1950s.*

Making a success of traditional tastes

Have you got any sucky sweets, mum?' Many a long car ride has been made more enjoyable by popping in a boiled sweet and happily sucking away on the confectionery to make the journey that bit more enjoyable. As the aeroplane rises through the clouds, mum doles out the sweets out once more, to make sure that our ears do not pop or hurt as the pressure changes. But it is not just to make a trip better that we eat pear drops and barley sugar, we do it because we like them. They are the traditional confectionery of the Briton. The Swiss can have their chocolate, we have got the likes of Pells Quality Confectionery. Humbug was the favourite word of old Scrooge, but to the confectioner it is the striped minty toffee that no other nation seems able to match. Acid drops, butterscotch and fruit drops belong as much to the modern era as they do to our childhood. You cannot beat traditions that continue to be relevant to the up to date society. We all love our sweets and thank goodness for companies like Pells that still believe in old, but not old-fashioned, recipés.

The Pell family began making boiled sweets in 1885, around the Commercial Road area. There the family business continued through three generations, including a move to the present premises on Conway Road in 1959. The business was sold in the mid 1980s and had four different owners after that. The latest one, Roy Allen, took it over in 1997. He has been able to carry on the blending of sugar, glucose, colouring and flavouring in the same time-honoured way. The mixtures are still produced in open copper pans, bubbling contentedly on the hob, filling the air with delightful and mouth-watering aromas. The happy band of employees are proud that their product is a quality one. The company I s one of only three still producing wrapped pear drops. Hoping to expand the gift pack and holiday gift side of the business, Pells knows that you will take pleasure in tickling your taste buds with that special bit of Welsh tradition.

Above: Just one of the company's famous labels.
Below: An early Pell's delivery lorry.

Miles of bunting and garlands turned Commercial Street into a riot of colour when King George VI was crowned on 12th May 1937.

This photograph may have been taken somewhere along the route which King George VI took when he visited Newport at the beginning of his Coronation tour in July 1937.

Acknowledgments

Mr. Gerry Keighley, Editor, The Newport Argus; Mr. Tom Ellis, former Assistant Editor, The Newport Argus; Photographs kindly reproduced from the collection held by Newport Museum and Art Gallery; special thanks to Mr. Bob Trett and his colleagues, Rachel Anderton and Mike Morgan; last but not least, Nancy and Gordon at the Beechwood Guest House, Chepstow Road for their endless patience and enthusiasm for the project

Thanks are also due to Margaret Wakefield who penned the editorial text and Andrew Mitchell and Mike Kirke for their copywriting skills